JAPANESE COOKING

日本料理

JAPANESE COOKING

日本料理

JON SPAYDE

Introduction by Emi Kazuko

CHARTWELL
BOOKS. INC.

A QUARTO BOOK

Published by Chartwell Books Inc.,
A Division of Book Sales Inc.,
110 Enterprise Avenue
Secaucus, New Jersey 07094
ISBN 0-89009-822-0

This book was designed and produced by
Quarto Publishing Limited
32 Kingly Court
London W1

Editor Lucinda Montefiore

Art editor Moira Clinch

Art director Alistair Campbell
Editorial director Christopher Fagg
Editorial assistant Michelle Newton
Photographers Michael Freeman, John Heseltine, James Stewart
Illustrator Robert Shone

Filmset by QV Typesetting Limited, London
Origination by Hong Kong Graphic Arts Service Center Limited, Hong Kong
Printed by Leefung Asco Printers Limited, Hong Kong

Quarto would like to extend special thanks to Emi Kazuko for her invaluable help
and advice

Quarto would also like to acknowledge the help of the following people and
organizations:
Takao Masuda and his team of chefs from the Benkay Restaurant, Hong Kong;
Hooraiya Restaurant, Hong Kong; Nadaman Restaurant, Shangri-La Hotel, Hong
Kong; Mr Iwamoto (Manager), Mr Fujimoto (Head Chef) and his team of chefs
from the Suntory Restaurant, London; Mr T. Hatakeyama; Miura Foods,
Kingston-upon-Thames; Peter Reed; Debbie Riviere; Carol Suffling; Karen
Gunner

CONTENTS

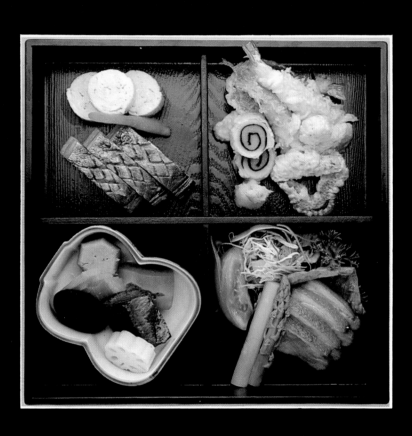

FOREWORD

*W*hen I first read Jon Spayde's manuscript I was struck by the fact that a gaijin ('foreigner' in Japanese) could have such insight into the culinary world of Japan. As a Japanese food writer and cook living abroad, I have all too often found myself irritated and disappointed by phoney 'Japanese' cookery books written by foreigners and displayed on the shelves of prestigious bookshops. Times are changing, and there is now developing a far more serious and informed interest in Japanese food among non-Japanese writers.

So what are the special qualities of Japanese cuisine? For Japanese people the most essential aim in cooking is to make food look and taste as natural as possible. When I introduced an English friend to Japanese green tea, she exclaimed 'Oh no! It's green!' and refused to taste it. I recall feeling quite patriotic towards our precious tea and saying to my friend 'What do you think the natural color of tea leaves is?' To me, drinking green tea leaves while they are green looks more natural and makes more sense than burning them brown and drinking them with milk and sugar.

I am particularly pleased to introduce this book because I think it has understood the special qualities — the essential simplicity and elegance — of Japanese cuisine. In the book you will find a range of authentic recipes from basic dishes to fascinating regional variations. If you find some a little challenging, you will also find many recipes that are hearteningly easy to make. And if, just like home cooks in Japan, you are ready to take a few short cuts, you will discover that Japanese cooking is not nearly as complicated and intimidating as some people would have you believe. I think this book presents an excellent opportunity for everyone to learn about real Japanese cooking, and it will enable you to cook and enjoy delicious Japanese food at home.

江見和子

EMI KAZUKO

THE SPIRIT OF JAPAN

Anyone with the slightest knowledge of Japan is aware of the Japanese sensitivity to nature; anyone who has tried Japanese food as it should be cooked and eaten knows that this sensitivity is powerfully expressed at the table. The genius of Japanese cooking is the subtle marrying of a few simple flavoring agents (fish stock, soysauce, *sake*) with the natural goodness of fresh ingredients. The art of garnishing seeks to remind each person that every piece of fish or chicken presented on a plate began its life in the open air. A sprig of *kinome* leaves or a cluster of pine needles decorating a dish evokes the bright greenness of the outdoor world where fish are caught and mushrooms gathered.

Regional Cookery

But the Japanese love of nature is more than an abstract love of the outdoors. It is one of the most powerful of all Japanese traits: a feeling for the particular, the concrete, and the local — for the real circumstances that surround people and things. Their many foods, cooked with simplicity and elegance, remind them not only of 'Japan' but of specific cities, regions, rivers, stretches of coastline. For the urban lover of good food, a trip to the countryside can be a gastronomic geography lesson; while the thousands of rural folk who flow into Tokyo from the Japanese North — and into the Ōsaka region from the South — enjoy tasty nostalgia in the numerous regional restaurants of these great cities.

In fact 'regional' Japanese cooking has come to be something of a paradox. Regional specialties have been available in the big cities for several centuries now, and Japanese people certainly approach their food from a 'regional' point of view. At the same time, Japan is too small and her cuisine too unified to sustain great separate regional traditions such as can be found in China. Japanese regional gastronomy is, rather, a matter of variations, emphases, and subtle permutations of a few national themes.

I like to compare Japanese cuisine with Japanese poetry. Classical verse begins with a few simple forms: the 31 syllable *tanka* of the court poets; the 17- and 14-syllable lines of the medieval poets, and the alternating five- and seven-syllable lines of dramatic poetry. The Japanese used these poetry-forms to reveal the real world, without imposing upon that world, distorting it or smothering it in 'poetic' sauce. Like fine Japanese cooks, they focused upon subject matter and paid attention to the ingredients. Their poems are always linked to real places, real events and the changing seasons, as is Japanese eating.

Indeed, the true aim behind the simplicity of Japanese cookery is to let the ingredients reveal their own particular beauty. Japanese regional cookery therefore begins with regional ingredients — with

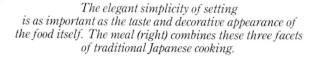

*The elegant simplicity of setting
is as important as the taste and decorative appearance of
the food itself. The meal (right) combines these three facets
of traditional Japanese cooking.*

Only 16 percent of Japan's total area is cultivable, and about half of this is given over to the rice crop, which is grown in the terraced paddy fields that characterize much of the landscape of central Japan. Since Japan is predominantly mountainous, most of the agriculture of Japan huddles onto a narrow strip of eastern coastland on the main island (above).

different areas of Japan famous for particular types of fish, vegetables, rice and tea. Unfortunately, much of the best regional food must remain inaccessible to those who cannot sample it at its point of origin. Since freshness is the one unbreakable rule of Japanese gastronomy, it is impossible to export the simplest — and perhaps the finest — regional dishes, which depend on the rapid preparation of freshly gathered produce.

Yet the 'regionality' of Japanese food goes deeper than the eating of an exotic specimen like the *hatahata* fish of the North. Various local ingredients are available in Japanese food shops in the West; certain regional techniques can be adapted handsomely to Western kitchens; and even the most familiar Japanese dishes originate from a particular locality. Knowing the geographical background of these foods can deepen anyone's experience of Japanese food. I don't know if the food tastes better when we begin to 'think regionally', but I am certain that it helps to make a Japanese meal even more of an adventure than it is to begin with.

There is a further reason to enjoy Japanese food from the regional point of view — and to me it is the best one of all. It can make any cook aware of his or her surroundings. Far from being an exercise in exoticism, Japanese cooking is a lesson in looking about you for what is good, fresh, and seasonal. The best way to cook in the Japanese spirit is to do just that — to learn as much of the spirit

of the cuisine as possible, then apply that spirit in one's own circumstances. The variety of subtle regional emphases and specialties shows, as nothing else can, the adaptability of the Japanese tradition. If you have no sea-bream handy, a fresh trout from the nearest river will broil beautifully, too — and you are already building something of a regional tradition in the Japanese spirit.

Natural Produce

It is rather odd that the Japanese should have the reputation for being dainty, over-refined cooks and eaters, fanciers of exquisite 'canapés' and little else. The fact is that food is a matter of great earnestness in Japan. The green tiers of paddy land hacked into ancient mountainsides over generations are evidence of a battle to squeeze the last grain of rice out of the beautiful but not overly generous Japanese earth. In some places, where the earth has been made to yield in abundance, such as northern Honshū, green oceans of rice wave in the wind, and one ancient poetic name for Japan — 'Land of Fertile Rice-Ears' — comes to life. In older, more densely populated western Japan, tiny paddies of every imaginable shape crowd right up to the roadways; there is emerald green wherever someone has not thought to put a building. Rice is more than a staple to the Japanese — it is the promise and symbol of nourishment itself. *Gohan* ('boiled rice') also means a meal, and,

The emerald-green tea bushes that wind in serpentine rows over the low hills are another characteristic sight of the Japanese agricultural landscape (above). The harvest season starts in May, and the gatherers still wear traditional, cone-shaped straw hats. Unlike Western tea, which is black, Japanese tea, or nihon-cha, is green and is an indispensable part of the Japanese diet.

Rivers in Japan are relatively short, and because of the steeply graded terrain, tend to be swift-flowing (left). This makes them highly suited to salmon and trout-fishing.

The swelling sails of fishing boats on Lake Kasumi (above). Fish is more important to the Japanese diet than meat.

except for the odd snack of a bowl of noodles, a meal without rice is a sort of contradiction in terms.

In contrast to the land, the sea surrounding Japan teams with edible produce. The warm, northerly Japan Current meets colder water flowing south from Siberia, and the turbulence that results creates a feeding ground of unparalleled richness; marine minerals cannot settle to the sea floor, and, instead, help to make Japanese ocean fish the best-tasting and most nourishing in the world. If the spawn of the swift rivers is added to the total, it is fair to estimate that the Japanese consume about one thousand varieties of fish and shellfish. In addition, there is a great harvest of iron-rich sea vegetables like kelp (*konbu*) and laver (*nori*), all of which play an important part in good cooking.

The Elements of Taste
The basic flavoring agents that make food 'taste Japanese' come from both sea and land. From the sea come the bonito (*katsuo*) and *nori* seaweed, which are used to brew the simple stock (*dashi*) — the basis of so many Japanese soups and simmering liquids. From rice comes the sacred drink of god and men, *sake*, also a vital cooking ingredient. Of Japanese land vegetables, incomparably the most important is the soybean (*daizu*), used to make soysauces of varying richness, *tōfu* (bean curd cakes), and hundreds of different

sorts of rich, yeasty *miso*. From Japan's many swift rivers comes pure, fresh water — essential to the preparation of Japanese food. Plenty of water is what removes the 'fishy' taste from *sashimi* (raw fish) and makes green tea truly tasty; and everything, except for deep-fried dishes, is cooked in water or a water-based medium.

Water, *dashi*, soysauce, *sake* and *miso* — these simple, delicious ingredients are applied to fresh foods, using one of the seven basic Japanese cooking techniques: raw fish-cutting, soup-making, broiling, steaming, simmering, deep-frying and 'saucing' (for salads); the result — Japanese food. Of course, it is not as simple as that, but simplicity is very much to the point. A French chef, visiting Japan, put it well when he wrote:

'With Japanese cooks...it looks as if they have had no higher ambition, for some thousand years or more, than to protect the flesh of fishes and the herbs of the fields from overcooking.'

For the Japanese, such an ambition is a high one indeed. While the Japanese today are not particularly religious, they are imbued with a feeling of awe before the natural world: the mountains, densely carpeted with evergreens; the sea, wrinkled and sparkling; the sheen of fresh-washed burdock root, and the iridescent shimmer along the side of a newly-caught *tai* (sea bream). To preserve freshness in cooking and to enhance texture by garnishing and arrangement are the twin goals of Japanese cooking.

Cormorant fishing (above) on Nagara River at Gifu. The light of burning braziers on the boat's prow attracts the ayu fish (a small river trout) to the surface. Trained cormorants dive beneath the surface to catch them, but rings around the birds' necks prevent them from swallowing the fish, which are disgorged and served immediately, either raw or broiled.

EATING OUT JAPANESE STYLE

A formal banquet is a gourmet tour of all the major techniques of Japanese cooking. The first stage of this culinary feast is the presentation, one after the other, of hors d'oeuvre, a clear soup and raw fish. Japanese gourmets think of the raw fish (*sashimi*) course as the high point of the meal and all the food that follows as a sort of long, graceful coda.

IN THE SECOND STAGE, the diner is presented with a broiled dish, a steamed dish, a simmered dish and something deep-fried in succession. If a one-pot is on the menu, it stands in for all four of these courses. A salad follows. To round off the banquet, white rice, *miso* soup and pickles are served together. A good grade of green tea and perhaps a piece of fruit end the meal.

A more detailed breakdown of how a large formal banquet is organized is illustrated right. Although you probably will not want to mount such a feast very often, if ever, it should show how 'modular' formal Japanese eating is.

Home cooks who wish to honour special guests will often prepare an abbreviated version of the formal bill of fare; a soup to begin with (either clear or *miso* based), a salad, and *sashimi*; then either a broiled or a deep-fried dish followed by something simmered or steamed. Tea, rice and pickles, together make up the final course.

If you visit Japan and are lucky enough to have a Japanese friend to introduce you to a fine restaurant there, you are assured of an unforgettable culinary experience. Short of that, however, a visit to a good Japanese restaurant in the West will present you with novel and delightful ways of eating.

Many Japanese restaurants abroad now feature a *sushi* bar where patrons sit, and behind which one or more *sushi* chefs prepare the rice sandwiches to order. You can sit at a table and order *sushi* from a waitress too, if you wish, but the food seems to taste better when you are perched at the bar, with the bright fish spread out before you, and the chef eager to introduce you to new textures and tastes.

Restaurants with *tempura* bars are more difficult to find abroad, but if you are lucky enough to run across one, you can enjoy this delicacy as it is meant to be eaten. While you sit at the bar, the chef will swirl your choice of ingredients in batter, fry them immediately and serve them piping hot in just minutes.

Larger restaurants offer small rooms, which are perfect for small parties and groups of friends. You will be attended by a waitress whose job is to introduce you to unfamiliar foods and cooking techniques. If you have ordered a *nabemono* (one-pot), *sukiyaki* or any of the other cook-it-yourself dishes, she will hover helpfully, either cooking the food for you or checking that you are doing it correctly. Do not be afraid to ask her questions. The Japanese are proud of their cuisine and love to help newcomers to enjoy it to the full.

1. *Zensai* (hors d'oeuvre) — tiny tidbits of seasonal vegetables or other delicacies
2. *Sumashi-jiru* (clear soup)
3. *Sashimi* (raw fish), with appropriate garnish and dipping sauces

4. *Yakimono* (broiled dish)
5. *Mushimono* (steamed dish)
6. *Nimono* (simmered dish)
7. *Agemono* (deep-fried dish)

A *nabemono* (one-pot dish) may stand in for the four above.

8. *Sunomono* or *aemono* (vinegared or dressed salad).

The three below are served together.
9. *Gohan* (boiled rice)
10. *Miso-shiru* (*miso*-based soup)
11. *Tsukemono* (pickles)

12. Green tea
13. Fresh fruit (optional)

A Formal Banquet

1. Hors d'oeuvre

2. Clear soup

3. Raw fish

4. Broiled dish

A one-pot dish may stand in for 4, 5, 6 & 7

6. Simmered dish

5. Steamed dish

7. Deep-fried dish

8. Vinegared salad

9. Rice 10. Miso soup 11. Pickles

12. Green tea

13. Fresh fruit

日本料理の基礎

THE
FUNDAMENTALS

UTENSILS

*T*he Japanese have not refined their kitchen equipment down to the amazing simplicity of the Chinese, who need little more than a *wok*, a few knives and a steamer to produce the world's most varied cuisine. Yet, there is no need to be put off at the outset by fears that Japanese cuisine requires shelves and shelves of arcane implements. It does not. The average Japanese kitchen is a cramped affair with a single gas burner, a miniature refrigerator and a narrow sink. Your own kitchen is probably already adequately supplied for making nine out of ten Japanese dishes. The following descriptions of the chief Japanese implements are meant to guide you in searching for the originals or in choosing the appropriate Western equivalents.

As in all cuisines, knives and pots represent a substantial investment of money; the rest of the Japanese utensils, even in import shops, are not expensive luxuries, and are generally reasonably-priced, hard-working objects. You can easily begin cooking in the Japanese style straight away, adding implements as you go, and as your skill and interest deepen.

Kitchen Carver (*deba-bōchō*): This is a versatile cleaver, used for basic fish and chicken cutting. Medium and large-size *deba-bōchō* (7 to 12in long) are used both for cleaving and for delicate boning operations. A combination of a medium-weight cleaver (capable of cutting bone) and a light French knife will handle most *deba-bōchō* tasks. A *ko-deba-bōchō* is a small version of a *deba-bōchō*, used for shellfish.

Vegetable Knife (*nakiri-bōchō*): Despite its appearance, this is not a cleaver, but a vegetable knife capable of doing everything the Japanese cook needs to do with vegetables, from chopping to delicate paring. It is light and swift and there is no close equivalent in the Western kitchen.

Fish Slicer (*sashimi-bōchō*): A Western meat-slicer can do the same job as this narrow knife which cuts fine strips and fish fillets — it is generally used in the making of *sashimi*.

Bean Curd Knife (*tōfu-bōchō*): Like a cake cutter, this is just the right instrument for slicing *tōfu*, or any other delicate job. However, *tōfu* may also be sliced by gently pressing straight through using any straight-bladed knife.

Chopsticks (*o-hashi*): Once you know how to use them, the Far Eastern 'knife and fork' are extremely helpful in the kitchen. A very long pair (preferably metal sticks with wooden handles) are best for deep-frying; intermediate-length wood or bamboo kitchen-chopsticks are perfect for handling simmered and steamed foods; and you will be surprised how easy it is to make a beautiful arrangement of food with a pair of ordinary paper-packaged table chopsticks.

Drop-Lid (*otoshi-buta*): This simple device is the technical secret behind the goodness of Japanese simmered food (*nimono*). Fitting easily inside a straight-sided saucepan, the wooden *otoshi-buta* gently rides on top of the food being simmered, making certain that the food is completely immersed. By 'holding' delicate ingredients in this way, the lid also protects them from being 'bruised' or broken by the boiling water.
U Unfortunately, these inexpensive items are rarely imported and they are difficult to find even in Oriental food or goods stores. A circle of baking-paper can be substituted, but for the serious Japanese-style cook, the *otoshi-buta* is something worth ordering by mail through a Japanese food or gift dealer.

Steamer (*mushiki*): Japanese steamers are round or square, made of metal, and quite expensive. A round bamboo steamer of the Chinese type is not only very reasonably priced, it is superior to the

Japanese type in one important way — moist bamboo is a far better insulator than metal, and so more steam-heat is retained. By all means invest in one of these useful contrivances; it will handle all your Japanese-style steaming requirements handsomely.

Grater (*oroshi-gane*): When really fine grating must be done, especially of *daikon*

(white radish) or *wasabi* root for condiments, this is the utensil for the job. The finest teeth of a Western-style grater will handle *daikon* and other vegetables, but when it comes to grating the ubiquitous *wasabi*, the *oroshi-gane* cannot be replaced.

Bamboo Draining Basket (*zaru*): The Japanese 'basket' is an all-purpose strainer and

A selection of kitchen knives:
1. Kitchen carvers (deba-bōchō)
2. Fish slicers (sashimi-bōchō) — the rectangular one is used in the Kansai
3. Vegetable knife (nakiri-bōchō)
4. All-purpose knife (banno-bōchō) used for decorative cutting and all kinds of chopping

drainer. While a combination of a colander and Western strainer works equally well, this is a handsome implement, in which noodles, for instance, may be served as well as strained.

Rice-Tub (*handai*): This is another handsome item that is not strictly necessary; one can serve rice in anything that retains heat. But, the sight of a round wooden rice tub filled with white steaming rice is very inviting and adds a nice authentic touch to a typical Japanese meal.

Japanese Omelet Pan (*makiyaki-nabe*): This small, oblong omelet pan is, on the other hand, absolutely necessary if one intends to cook egg dishes such as *dashimaki* ('rolled egg'). There is simply no other pan suitable for making this small, tidy, oblong omelet which is rolled as it is sautéed. Good omelet pans for the private kitchen are made of heavy copper, tin-coated, and should be seasoned with a little oil before use; they are available in the better Oriental goods stores.

Bamboo Mat (*sudare*): This is another useful one-purpose implement, used in rolling up *nori-maki* ('seaweed-roll') *sushi* and 'rolled egg'.

Skimmer (*ami-shakushi*): The deep-frying cook uses this skimmer to clear bits of fried batter from his/her oil. This important job can be accomplished equally well by a

slotted spoon of the Western type.

Mortar/Pestle (*suribachi/ surikogi*): The Japanese name for a mortar literally means 'grinding bowl', and it is a clever name because the bowl itself helps in the grinding. It is scored on the inside with hundreds of tiny grooves. When the wooden pestle is used, the inside of the *suribachi* acts as a grater, breaking up kernels and seeds with amazing efficiency. A wooden pestle often comes with the *suribachi*, but if you have to buy one, choose a long one as this will provide good leverage.

Fan (*uchiwa*): Gentle swings of this fan keep a charcoal broiler glowing.

Skewers (*gushi*): Japanese broiling is done over charcoal, usually with skewers. Long, metal ones (15in) are perhaps the most versatile for whole-fish broiling, while the small 8in bamboo skewers are used for chicken *yakitori*. There are also many intermediate sizes. Metal skewers should be kept sharp and rust-free.

Tempura Pot (*tempura-nabe*): Complete with draining rack, this pot makes tempura-making a little easier, chiefly because it is ideally designed

for keeping oil at an even temperature. A Chinese *wok*, despite what manufacturers or importers may say, is not an ideal *tempura* pot. The genius of the *wok* is the fact that is maintains several different temperatures at different points on its surface, so it is unpredictable when filled with oil. Instead of a *tempura-nabe*, use a thick, straight-sided pot.

Earthenware Casserole (*do-nabe*): A useful pot made of earthenware, it can be placed directly over an open flame (if its outside surface is perfectly dry) in the preparation of Japan's delicious one-pot dishes (*nabemono*).

Transferred directly to table, it is an attractive addition to table decor. Although fragile, it spreads and maintains even heat very well.

Stewing Pot (*tetsu-nabe*): This is an iron pot with a wooden lid, perfect for holding hearty, northern stews and ragoûts.

Shallow Cast-Iron Pan (*sukiyaki-nabe*): This is a traditional, flattish pan used for *sukiyaki*. It is flat because *sukiyaki* is a fried/sautéed one-pot dish, in contrast to its cousin *shabu-shabu*, where ingredients boil in plenty of water.

Iron Griddle (*teppan*): This is a large flat 'iron sheet' used for cooking the modern dish, *teppan-yaki*, where ingredients are broiled on a griddle in front of the customers.

Skillet (*oyako-nabe*): An intriguingly-shaped little skillet — the handle sticks straight up. This arrangement allows the cook to swirl the egg about easily as he or she makes the spiralled chicken-omelet that sits atop rice in the popular dish, *oyako-domburi*. A small pancake pan is a good substitute.

INGREDIENTS

The purpose of the list below is to provide a guide to ingredients essential to Japanese cooking. Some of these ingredients can easily be obtained in the West; other less familiar items can be found in Japanese, Indian or Chinese food stores; for ingredients difficult to obtain, substitutes have been indicated when possible.

In most cases, both the romanized Japanese names and their English equivalents have been given. Common usage has dictated whether the English or Japanese name should be used throughout the book.

Bamboo shoots (*takenoko*): In Japan, fresh shoots appear on the market in the spring. Instructions for boiling and preserving fresh bamboo shoots are given on page 78. Canned bamboo shoots are a rather poor second choice, but if you do have to use them, you can keep them fresh by covering them with cold water (which should be changed daily) and storing them in the fridge.

Bonito flakes, dried (*katsuo-bushi*): Fillets of the bonito, a member of the mackerel family, are dried to make a solid block of bonito. The finest *dashi* is made with flakes shaved from this solid block. However, the difficulty of obtaining a bonito block, and the skill required to 'shave' it, make pre-flaked bonito a necessity for most cooks outside Japan. Packaged dried bonito flakes are called *hana-katsuo* and are widely available in Japanese stores; they are sold in cellophane bags which come in a variety of sizes. Freshness is important, so ask your grocer to confirm the date of packing (which should be stamped on the label, and will be written in Japanese).

Burdock (*gobō*): This is a long, slender, irregularly-shaped root vegetable whose crunchy texture and ability to absorb the flavors of simmering juices and sauces make it a mainstay of Japanese cuisine. Fresh burdock should be trimmed (little rootlets may be present), washed and scrubbed with a brush, but not peeled. After slicing, it should be immersed in cold water so that its color is retained. Oriental specialty grocers generally carry both the fresh root and a pre-boiled, canned variety.

Chrysanthemum leaves (*shungiku*): These greens, delicious and very high in Vitamin A, are used in many one-pots and other dishes. Most Oriental markets carry them during the fall months, when they are at their best.

Daikon (large Japanese white radish): The English word 'radish' hardly does justice to this imposing vegetable, which can grow to a length of 14in and a weight of 5lb. It is a versatile ingredient in stews and soups, in one-pots and simmered dishes. The thick, fibrous flesh of the *daikon* requires relatively long cooking. Its most familiar use, however, is as a raw garnish: *daikon-oroshi*, or grated *daikon*, where it adds tang to dipping sauces. White Western radish or Chinese white radish may be substituted, but the tiny pink bulb which is what is usually meant by a 'radish' is *not* usable.

Dashi (fish and seaweed-based soup stock): *Dashi* is as important to Japanese cuisine as butter is to French cuisine and olive oil to Italian. When something 'tastes Japanese', no matter how simple, the flavor probably comes from this stock, accented with soy-sauce. *Dashi* is hot water flavored with *konbu* (kelp) and flakes of bonito (*katsuo-bushi*), which are strained out before the *dashi* is used.

All Japanese food stores sell *dashi* essence in little 'tea-bags' under the name *dashi-nomoto*. The stock that results is quite good, but you may well choose to make a slightly fresher version. *Dashi* made from 'scratch' is called primary, or *ichiban dashi*, while secondary *dashi* (*niban dashi*) is made from bonito and *konbu* that have already been used for making the primary type stock. *Ichiban dashi* is mainly used for clear soups while *niban dashi* is best-suited for heavier stews and noodle broths.

Eggplant (*nasu*): All Japanese eggplant varieties are smaller than those found in the West. The most common variety is sweeter and less watery than the Western eggplant; the small eggplants available in Asian food stores shops can be substituted.

Enokitake ´mushrooms:
Used in soups and one-pots, these mushrooms are very distinctive with their whitish-yellow stems and their minute round caps. They have a mild, pleasant flavor and aroma, and a crisp texture.

Ginger (*shōga*): Fresh ginger is widely available in food stores. Dried, powdered ginger is not appropriate for Japanese cuisine. To use fresh ginger, break off a knob and pare the skin away from as much as you are likely to need; ginger juice can be obtained by squeezing freshly grated ginger.

   Three types of prepared ginger, delicious and widely used, are available in Japanese specialty grocers. Vinegared ginger comes in two forms: *gari*, which is yellowish and used as a *sushi* garnish, and *beni-shōga*, which is dyed a bright pink. *Hajikami-shōga*, literally 'blushing ginger', refers to pickled ginger shoots. These shoots are bright red in color and have a pungent taste; they

---

MAKING DASHI

ICHIBAN DASHI
4¹/₂ cups (34fl.oz) water
1oz konbu
1oz dried bonito flakes
(katsuo-bushi)

Put 4 cups (32fl.oz) cold water into a large saucepan and add 1oz *konbu*. Heat the water and, just before it boils, remove the *konbu*. Allow the water to come to a full boil, then add ¼ cup (2fl.oz) cold water to bring the temperature down quickly. Immediately add 1oz bonito flakes. Let the mixture return to the boil, then boil the flakes for only 2 or 3 seconds; any longer, and the stock will become bitter. Remove from the heat and strain.

NIBAN DASHI
konbu and bonito flakes
reserved from ichiban
dashi
6 cups (48fl.oz) cold water
¹/₂oz dried bonito flakes

Place the *konbu* and bonito flakes reserved from *ichiban dashi* into 6 cups (48fl.oz) cold water and heat just to boiling point. Lower the heat and simmer the contents for about 20 minutes, or until the stock is reduced by half. Add ¹/₂oz dried bonito flakes to the stock and remove the saucepan from the heat. Leave to stand for 30 seconds to 1 minute, then strain the *dashi* through a sieve lined with cheesecloth.

---

are ideal as garnishes for strongly flavored foods like broiled meat.

Ginkgo nut (*ginnan*):
Ginkgo nuts can be purchased canned in specialty food stores, and are also available fresh during the fall months. Fresh nuts should be cracked with a knife or nutcracker, and the

hard outer nut case removed; then the nuts should be placed in hot (not boiling) water to loosen a thin brownish inner skin. This skin should then be rubbed away. Ginkgo nuts are used to add flavor to *chawan-mushi* and other steamed food; if *chawan-mushi* becomes a personal favorite of yours, it is well worth seeking out the fresh nuts, as canned nuts have little flavor.

Harusame ('Spring rain' filaments): These fine, near-transparent, white noodles are made from rice or potato flour. They are often used in one-pot dishes and need to be soaked for about 5 minutes in hot water before use.

Kamaboko (fish paste): *Kamaboko* is made by adding a starchy binding agent to puréed white fish, molding the mixture into shape, then steaming it. The most familiar type is molded into a Nissen-hut shape, tinted pink or light green, and placed on a small piece of cypress wood. This 'plank' *kamaboko* (*ita-kamaboko*) is sold in 7oz cakes and is widely available in Japanese food shops. *Kamaboko* is an important ingredient in *oden* (see page 185) and other stews.

Kinome: A general term for young leaves, that are used widely as garnishes in Japanese cooking. The fragrant sprig of the *sansho* tree is particularly popular, both as a garnish and for seasoning.

Konbu (dried kelp): This dark greenish-brown sea vegetable is an important flavoring agent for *dashi*. The white mold that lightly dusts its surface contributes to its sweetish flavor, and should not be rubbed or washed away. *Konbu* is sold dried, in cellophane packs and every Japanese grocer carries it.

Dried *konbu* may be stored at room temperature in a dry, airtight container. *Konbu* that has been reserved from making *dashi* will keep 3 or 4 days in a refrigerator, tightly covered with a plastic wrap.

Konnyaku: This gelatinous, pearly grey cake is processed from the root of a vegetable called 'devil's tongue'. Like *tōfu* and burdock, it has little taste of its own, but absorbs liquids and their flavors readily. It is available in Japanese grocers, and is sometimes labelled 'yam cake' or 'alimentary paste'. *Konnyaku* keeps for about 2 weeks if covered with water, and if the water is changed daily.

Kuzu starch: An all-purpose thickener for soups and stews, this starch is extracted from the root of the *kuzu* vine, a wild plant which is very common in Japan. *Kuzu* starch not only gives soups and stews a glossy 'finish', it is also a fine coating for deep-fried foods. It is expensive, however, and cornstarch can be substituted. *Kuzu* is available in most Japanese specialty grocers.

Matsutake mushrooms: The *matsutake*, with its stem as thick and succulent as beef, and its savor of fragrant piney woods, is one of the greatest Japanese delicacies. Since these mushrooms cannot be successfully cultivated commercially (they only grow in red-pine forests), they are costly and can be difficult to obtain outside of Japan. Ask for

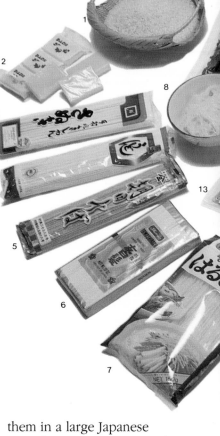

them in a large Japanese specialty grocers; you may be able to find the fresh article, imported in sawdust-filled crates. *Matsutake* are generally enjoyed on their own.

Mirin: Sweet cooking *sake* is one of the basic resources of the Japanese cook. *Mirin* lends its sweetness to many simmering liquids, glazes and dipping sauces. All Japanese grocery stores carry it, but you will not find it in liquor stores, as its alcoholic content is very low. If you cannot obtain it, substitute sugar in the ratio of 1 tsp to 1 tbsp *mirin*.

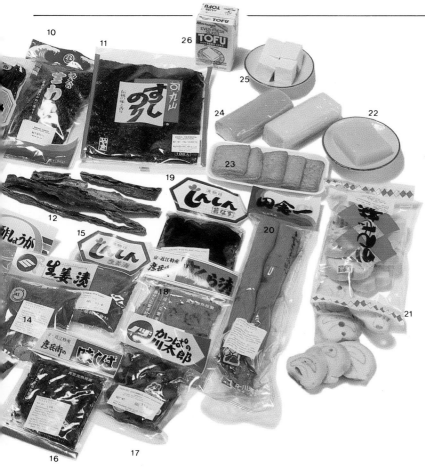

A selection of dried and packaged ingredients:
1. Kome (uncooked Japanese rice) 2. Mochi (glutinous rice cake) 3. Udon (white noodles) 4. Kishimen (flat noodles) 5. Soba (buckwheat noodles) 6. Sōmen (fine noodles) 7. Harusame ('spring rain' filaments) 8. Shirataki ('white waterfall' filaments) 9. Dried wakame seaweed 10. Fresh wakame seaweed 11. Nori seaweed (dried laver sheet) 12. Konbu (dried kelp) 13. Gari (pickled sweet and sour ginger slices), eaten with sushi 14. Beni-shōga shreds (vinegared ginger), also eaten with sushi 15. Beni-shōga slices 16-19. Japanese pickles 20. Takuan (pickled daikon) 21. Fu (wheat gluten) 22. Konnyaku (cake made from devil's tongue root) 23. Satsuma-age (fried fish paste) 24. Kamaboko (fish paste) 25. Fresh tōfu (bean curd) 26. Tōfu in a packet

Miso (fermented soybean paste): This is an inspired Japanese culinary invention. It is produced by boiling soybeans, mashing them, then adding rice, wheat or barley in varying proportions and combinations. The mixture is fermented by the introduction of a yeast-like mold. Used as a soup base, a salad dressing, a pickling medium and even a condiment (as in *dengaku*), *miso* comes in many varieties, thicknesses, and colors. Lighter *miso* is used in sauces and Kansai-style *miso* soup; darker varieties are better for richer soups and stews, as well as general cooking tasks. Yellow varieties, perhaps the most widely available, are good for general cooking.

Mochi (glutinous rice cake): *Mochi* rice cakes are produced by pounding glutinous rice (*mochigome*) in a large wooden mortar. The chewy white paste that results is shaped into round cakes, and these are eaten as they are, or lightly toasted. Nowadays, most *mochi* cakes are processed commercially and sold ready-made; they are available in Japanese grocers.

Nameko: These tiny button mushrooms are generally sold canned and are available in all Japanese food stores; they are often used in soups and one-pots.

Nori seaweed: This is the commonest and most useful of the many varieties of seaweed that the Japanese consume. *Nori*, often translated as 'laver', is used as a *sushi*-wrap and a garnish for many dishes. Dried *nori* should be freshened by a light toasting — pass the

A selection of condiments and seasonings: *1. Soysauce (shōyu) 2. Su (rice vinegar) 3. Mirin (sweet sake) 4. Aka-miso (dark fermented soybean paste) 5. Shiro-miso (light fermented soybean paste) 6. Tsubu-miso (coarse fermented soybean paste) 7. Katsu-bushi (dried bonito) 8. Hana-katsuo (dried bonito flakes) 9. Katsuo dashi nomoto (flavored soup stock) 10. Kuro-goma (black sesame seeds) 11. Shiro-goma (white sesame seeds 12. Wasabi powder (powdered Japanese horseradish) 13. Ao-nori (green nori flakes) 14. Sansho (ground sansho seeds) 15. Shichimi tōgarashi (Japanese pepper)*

standard-size sheet (8 × 7in) over a gas flame two or three times. Crumbled *nori* is sold in small bottles like pepper shakers; these *ao-nori* (green *nori* flakes) are shaken onto various dishes to add flavor.

Onions: There are two main types used in Japan — the *aonegi* and the *naganegi* ('long onion'). The *aonegi*, a small, slim green onion, is found largely in Kansai cooking. The *naganegi*, which reaches lengths of 14-16in, is most familiar in Tokyo and the North. With the *aonegi*, the green part is mainly used, with the *naganegi* the long white part. Both types of onion are difficult to obtain outside of Japan. You may substitute a green onion for the *aonegi* and a white onion for the

naganegi.

Red beans (*azuki* beans): These beans are identical to those that play an important part in Latin American cooking. In addition to making an appearance in red rice (see page 95), red beans are the basis of many Japanese sweets.

Renkon (lotus root): This crunchy vegetable appears in *tempura*, vinegared and simmered dishes. Generally cut into rounds, it has an attractive flower-like cross-section that is immediately recognizable. Since it discolors quickly after paring, it should be kept in a bath of lightly vinegared cold water until use. It is available both in Chinese and Japanese food shops. Choose the fresh or canned root; dried lotus is

Chinese and cannot be used as a substitute for fresh or canned *renkon* in Japanese cooking.

Sansho (prickly-ash powder): This spice, made by grinding the small yellowish seed-pods of the prickly ash tree, is unique to Japan, and is one of the most delicious seasonings of any cuisine. Available at all Japanese specialty grocers, *sansho* is usually sprinkled on meats.

Sesame (*goma*): Both white (*shiro-goma*) and black (*kuro-goma*) sesame seeds are used in Japanese cooking. Whether used whole or crushed, sesame seeds are lightly roasted beforehand, without oil. White seeds are often found in salads, while black ones are sprinkled over bowls of rice.

Shichimi tōgarashi ('seven-taste pepper'): This is a delicious condiment that the Japanese like to shake on to food at the last minute. It is a complex blend of red pepper, *sansho* pepper, ground orange peel, sesame seeds, hemp seeds, poppy seeds and ground *nori* seaweed. Available in Japanese specialty grocers, it is used to season many dishes, and it is also placed on the table so that everybody can add it to their soup or noodle broth.

Shiitake mushrooms: This is the 'standard' mushroom of Japanese cookery, also cultivated and enjoyed in Korea and China. Both dried and fresh *shiitake* are sold in Oriental grocery stores, and either type will do nicely for the recipes in this book. Select fresh mushrooms whose caps are fleshy and firm, and slightly curled under. The dried variety is generally sold in 1oz packages containing eight to 10 caps. Dried mushrooms must always be soaked prior to use, preferably for an hour or more, but at the very least for 30 minutes.

Shirataki: These transparent noodles, used in *sukiyaki*, are actually clear filaments made from the root of the devil's tongue plant, which is also the source of *konnyaku*. *Shirataki* are available both in water-filled cellophane bags and in cans in Oriental food stores. In either case, after removing the *shirataki*, you should rinse and

drain them to remove the slightly unpleasant odor they take on when packed.

Shishito pepper: This small green pepper, often used as a garnish, looks like a hot green chilli, but it is mild and sweet. Use a strip of green pepper as a substitute.

Soba (buckwheat noodles): *Soba* are sold dry in 18oz packages, and, less often, as fresh pasta in vacuum-sealed plastic packets. They are easy to obtain in Japanese specialty grocers. *Soba* are greyish-brown in color, except for the variety called *cha-soba* ('tea soba') — which are made with green tea.

Soysauce (*shōyu*): Japanese food would not be Japanese food without this rich, pungent sauce made from roasted soybeans, wheat and salt. It is used so often that it is important for the cook to know the right types to buy. There are two distinct types of soysauce: a dark, salty variety much favored in Chinese cooking but not used in Japan, and the sweeter, generally lighter Japanese varieties. With Japanese soysauce there is another distinction between dark and light. Dark soysauce is available in most grocers, but you will need to visit a Japanese store for the more expensive lighter type. Light soysauce is employed when the cook wants to avoid darkening the color of ingredients; it is saltier than the

dark type. It is best to buy it in small quantities, as exposure to light will eventually darken it. If you cannot find the light variety, dark soysauce is fine as a substitute.

In order to avoid buying inappropriate varieties, make certain that the soysauce you select has been made in Japan or by a Japanese concern.

Tōfu (bean curd): The milky-white, custard-like bean-curd cake is a Chinese invention. Soybeans are boiled and crushed, then a coagulant is added to form the curds. If the curds are then drained, the result is 'cotton' *tōfu*, the standard type; if they are not, a more delicate and fragile *tōfu* (called 'silk') is produced. 'Cotton' *tōfu*, the most readily available abroad, will do for all the recipes in this book; if you want to make a really elegant clear soup using *tōfu*, you might seek out the finer variety at your Japanese specialty grocers. In the West, fresh *tōfu* is invariably sold in water-filled plastic tubs, date-stamped to indicate freshness. *Yakidōfu*, light golden-brown broiled bean curd, is sold the same way. Because it is popular as a health food outside Japan, you may be able to find *tōfu* in large non-specialty grocers as well as Japanese stores. Store *tōfu* in plenty of cold water, under refrigeration; change the water every day.

Trefoil (*mitsuba*): This herb, a member of the parsley family, appears frequently in Japanese cuisine. Used either coarsely chopped, or whole, it is added both for its flavor and its decorative green color.

Udon (white noodles): Made of wheat flour, these hearty noodles are available in several thicknesses and lengths. Dried *udon* are packaged in 4oz individual portions, each of which yields about four or five servings. You can store dried noodles almost indefinitely, but if you are lucky enough to find the fresh variety at your Oriental market, use the noodles within two days of purchase.

Vinegar (*su*): Japanese rice vinegar is increasingly being used in other national cuisines around the world. The mild flavor of the light yellow vinegar is exactly right for salad dressings and dishes that call for pungency without harshness. Needless to say, it is the only sort of vinegar that should ever be used for Japanese cooking. Rice vinegar is available in bottles in Japanese specialty food stores, and in many gourmet food stores as well. A special variety, *sushi-su*, is seasoned for use in making sushu.

Wakame seaweed: This is a type of seaweed, called 'lobe-leaf' in English. Sold dry, it has a rather unappealing dusty-brown color. When soaked, however, it turns bright, rich green. *Wakame* leaves are stripped from the central vein along which they grow, and used as a salad garnish. *Wakame* is one of the most nutritious of all sea vegetables.

Wasabi horseradish: Called 'tears' (*namida*) in *sushi*-shop jargon, this paste is made from the powdered root of the *wasabi* plant and it is pungent enough to make you weep if you use too much. It is unlikely that you will be able to find the fresh root, even in the best Japanese food stores, but the powdered form is widely sold. To prepare, mix a small amount of water with a little powder until you get a smooth paste. *Wasabi* accompanies most raw fish dishes.

A selection of vegetables:
1. *Red beans (azuki beans)*
2. *Nameko mushrooms*
3. *Hoshi shiitake (dried Chinese mushrooms)*
4. *Burdock (gobō)*
5. *Renkon (lotus root) – a crunchy vegetable that appears in tempura, vinegared and simmered dishes*
6. *Canned burdock (gobō)*
7. *Daikon (Japanese white radish)*
8. *Leek – used as a substitute for naganegi (thin, long, green Japanese onion)*
9. *Green onion*
10. *Ginkgo nuts (ginnan)*
11. *Kinome (young leaves)*
12. *Takenoko (bamboo shoots)*

PREPARING FISH

While you can always ask your fishmonger to fillet fresh fish for you, you are missing an opportunity to come closer to the spirit of Japanese cooking if you do so. The Japanese love fish; they love to eat them, to look at them, to angle for them, to discuss their spawning habits and their special properties. Preparing fish from scratch for broiling, steaming or *sashimi* will make you increasingly sensitive to freshness, and increasingly familiar with the characteristics and excellences of fish available on the market. Find a reliable fishmonger and talk to him; he will be able to provide you with all sorts of information. There is no need to become an amateur marine biologist to learn about fish — you will soon become knowledgeable about the five or six you like best.

Roundfish and flatfish: *The shape of a fish determines the way it should be gutted and filletted. The sketches (right) show the two generalized fish types: roundfish and flatfish.*

As with all Japanese cooking, freshness is essential. In judging whole fish, remember that the viscera and gills are the first parts to decay. Sniff carefully. Nothing should offend your nose. Test the underbelly for springy firmness — a 'soft underbelly' means that the viscera are beginning to go. Check the fish's eyes — they should look as bright and clear as if the fish was about to leap out of your hands. The gills should be bright pink.

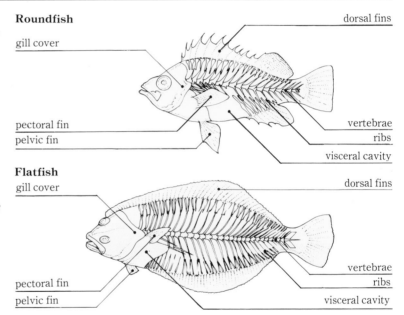

Roundfish
gill cover
dorsal fins
pectoral fin
pelvic fin
vertebrae
ribs
visceral cavity

Flatfish
gill cover
dorsal fins
pectoral fin
pelvic fin
vertebrae
ribs
visceral cavity

PREPARING WHOLE FISH

To maintain freshness, all fish should be gutted and have their gills removed as quickly as possible. The key to cleaning a fish that will be served whole is to do the utmost to preserve its shape.

Small fish, if they are very fresh, can be eviscerated through the mouth. Force open the fish's mouth, which will in turn open the gill flaps wide enough for you to insert the tip of your knife and sever the small bone below the fish's jaw. Then, insert first one, then another short wooden chopstick through the mouth to a point beyond the gills. Give the chopsticks a couple of turns, and carefully remove the viscera, which will be wound around the chopsticks. The gills also come out in the process.

For larger fish, cut a slit from just behind and below the gills to the anus on one side only, and carefully remove the innards. Wash the cavity with copious amounts of water. Another method for larger fish, slightly more tricky although it preserves the shape well, is to remove the viscera through a small slit near the pelvic fin.

To remove the gills, force open the fish's mouth and sever the bone beneath the gills. This will allow you to hold the gill slit open with thumb and forefinger, and sever the gills from the bone. Remove the gills carefully.

Cleaning and filleting fish:

There is nothing unusual or mysterious about the way that the Japanese fillet fish. The two main techniques are the sanmai-oroshi ('three-piece') and gomai-oroshi ('five-piece') methods. Sanmai-oroshi is used for roundfish only. This method yields two fillets and a lightly fleshed backbone (see this page). Gomai-oroshi is the standard method for filleting flatfish, and provides two 'double' fillets and a fleshy skeleton (see opposite). Do not discard the spine section in either case — broiled, it provides succulent pieces of meat.

Sanmai-oroshi: *1. First wash the whole fish in slightly salted water, then remove scales with short strokes, using a scraper or the back of a knife.*

2. Remove the head by making an incision just below the pectoral fin. Cut gently in a diagonal down to the spine on both sides.

3. To clean the fish, cut along the belly and remove the innards. Rinse the cavity thoroughly with cold water at intervals. Run the tip of the knife along the spine to remove blood pockets and rinse again.

4. Rest your free hand gently on top of the fish and draw a knife gently along the fish's spine. Make long, light strokes.

Retrace the cut more than once, going a little deeper toward the spine each time. Do not poke or saw the tender flesh.

5. Turn the fish and make an incision at the base of the tail down to the bone. Place a knife in this cut and cut smoothly right to left, lifting the fillet free as you go. Repeat this process on the other side of the fish.
Right: two boneless fillets and a lightly fleshed backbone.

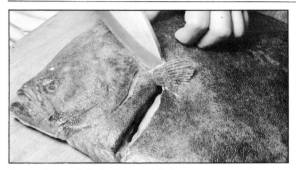

Gomai-oroshi: *1. Most flatfish need to be scaled on the upper side only. Having scaled the fish, place it on a cutting board and, with a kitchen carver, make two deep cuts behind the gills, as shown, to remove the head.*

2. Squeeze out the viscera by pressing on the upper part of the fish. Ease out any remaining bits in the central cavity with the tip of the knife. Rinse the fish thoroughly with cold water.

3. Then make an incision down the spine of the fish to the base of the tail, cutting to the bone. Place the edge of your knife in the spinal cut and, keeping your blade flat, cut along one side of the fish close to the dorsal fin toward the tail. Remove the fillet.

4. Reverse the fish and draw your knife along the other side. Remove the second fillet. Turn the fish over and repeat step 3, gently lifting the other two fillets free.
Below, the gomai-oroshi technique completed — four prepared fillets.

PREPARING VEGETABLES

*A*n excellent way to begin cooking Japanese-style is to try some of the decorative ways of cutting vegetables that help to make the Japanese plate or soup-bowl so pleasing to the eye. Even here, however, food is not being prepared whimsically or 'purely decoratively'. Pieces of vegetable are sliced and shaped with careful attention to how they will be treated in the finished dish. Thick pieces of sturdy vegetable are meant to stand up to stewing; compact pieces go into soup; and the most delicate cuts are reserved for vegetables that will be served lightly vinegared or raw, as garnish or decoration. Described in the following pages, are some standard ways of cutting, along with their colorful Japanese names. Practise them, for cleverly cut vegetables can brighten any dish, Eastern or Western.

Step-by-step illustrations for some of the more popular cuts are opposite and overleaf.

Rounds: This is the simple sidewise cut you probably already use for long vegetables like carrot. Rounds of *daikon* are also common in Japanese cooking.

Half-Moon Cut (*hangetsu-giri*): Cut any long vegetable in half lengthwise, then slice into rounds to make half-rounds.

Diagonal Cut (*sogi-giri*): The Japanese name means 'sharpening cut'. When peasants made bamboo spears to defend themselves against marauders, they cut the bamboo ends on a sharp diagonal to make a crude but effective spearhead. The diagonal cut is good for carrots, Japanese cucumber and long green onions.

Disordered Cut (*ran-giri*): This is a way of producing the sort of elegant randomness the Japanese like. Cut your long vegetable on the diagonal, but rotate it *one quarter turn* after each cut.

Bevel Edge: This is a good way of handling sturdy, large vegetables like sweet potato, *daikon* and turnip that will be cut into rounds and simmered. Cutting bevel edges helps the pieces keep their shape, since edges will not crumble.

Six-Sided Paring (*roppō-muki*): This is another good method of cutting large vegetables. Cut rounds, then carefully trim them into hexagons. If you want thinner hexagons, of course, you can slice crosswise as thinly as you wish.

Cube Cut (*sainome-giri*): Little ³/₈in cubes like tiny mah-jong dice. A direct translation of *sainome-giri* is 'dice-cut'.

Hail Cut (*arare-giri*): 'Dicing'. Very small cubes — even smaller than in the cut above. (Translations make for confusion!)

Molecule Cut (*mijin-giri*): Very fine chopping.

Poem-Card Cut (*shikishi-giri*): This cut is named after *shikishi*, brightly colored, nearly square cards upon which poems are written. With this cut, you slice off as many little 'poem cards' as you need.

Poetry-Paper Cut (*tanzaku-giri*): Here is further proof that my analogy between Japanese poetry and Japanese cooking is not too far-fetched. Divide your block of vegetable lengthwise to produce rectangles (or cut a rectangular section to begin with), and slice these. The cut is named after the *tanzaku*, another piece of paper upon which one writes a Japanese poem; the paper is a long rectangle, a handsome shape for flowing calligraphy.

Thousand-Cut (*sen-giri*): Make a little stack of thin *tanzaku* sections, and cut them finely lengthwise. The result is Japanese 'julienne'.

Clapper Cut (*hyōshigi-giri*): The shape of these vegetable rectangles recalls the clappers (wooden blocks) that were slapped together to announce the beginning of a *kabuki* play.

Sheet of Vegetable (*katsura-muki*): This is the only

Half-moon cut *(hangetsu-giri):*
Cut any long vegetable in half
lengthwise, then slice into rounds
to make half-rounds.

Quarter-moon cut: *Cut half-*
moon pieces in half. This cut is
used if the vegetable is very large.

Disordered cut *(ran-giri): Cut*
the vegetable into thick sticks. Cut
the sticks on a diagonal, but
rotate it one quarter turn after
each cut.

Six-sided paring *(roppo-muki):*
1. This cut is used to turn
vegetable rounds into hexagons.
Cut rounds, then pare the sides to
form hexagons.

2. If you want thinner hexagons
(to use as garnishes), slice the
hexagon shape crosswise as thinly
as you wish.

3. Thick hexagons are used largely
for soups, steamed and simmered
dishes.

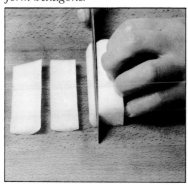

Dice cut *(sainome-giri): 1. Trim*
round any long vegetable to make
a square cross-section.

2. Then cut into cubes of equal
size to ensure even cooking.

Molecule cut *(mijin-giri): Very*
fine chopping. If the vegetable is
thick, cut into thin shreds first and
then chop very finely.

Poem-card cut *(shikishi-giri): 1. Cut a long block of vegetable into a square cross-section.*

2. Cut this cross-section into slices to the thickness you require. Thick slices are appropriate for cooked dishes, thin slices for garnishes.

Clapper cut *(hyōshigi-giri): 1. Cut the vegetable into 2in long pieces, and trim round to make a square cross-section.*

2. Slice lengthwise to ¼-½in thickness, then turn the piece over and cut to the same thickness.

Sheet-paring *(katsura-muki): 1. Hold a 3in length of daikon in the palm of one hand with your thumb on the edge of a sharp knife.*

2. Carefully controlling the knife with your thumb, peel the daikon very thinly until you get the length you require.

Twists *(yori-udo): 1. Place your sheet (see sheet-paring) on a cutting board and cut into thin strips.*

2. Place these thin strips in ice-cold water; they will curl in the water. These strips make a very pretty garnish.

Thunderclouds *(kaminari): 1. Roll up a thin daikon sheet (katsura-muki) as tightly as possible. Be careful not to split it.*

2. Slice crosswise as thinly as possible. The very thin curly filaments are used as a garnish for sashimi.

Fan cut *(ohgi-giri): 1. Make very thinly spaced slits length-wise on the bottom half of a 2 × 3in piece of vegetable.*

2. Using the blade of a knife, or your finger, press down where the slits begin to open and spread them into a fan.

Mountain shape *(yamagata): 1. Cut a long vegetable into 3in sections. Then make a cut through the center lengthwise.*

2. Make a diagonal cut half way down toward the central cut and do the same on the other side.

3. Pull both ends to separate the two pieces. You will have two mountain shaped vegetables.

Pineneedle *(matsuba): 1. This cut is suitable for long vegetables like cucumber and daikon. Quarter the vegetable to make sticks.*

2. With a sharp knife, peel back a little 1in strip of skin and, using an index finger, hold the peeled skin to the side.

3. Repeat this cut all the way round so that you make many little strips around the vegetable stick.

technique in the list that will take really diligent practice to master. It is a method of turning a 5 or 6in section of *daikon* or carrot into one, long, continuous, paper-thin sheet of vegetable. The Japanese *nakiri-bōchō* vegetable knife is the ideal size and weight for the job, but you can make a good, sharp, wide-bladed knife of any type work reasonably well. If successful, you will produce a truly beautiful piece of vegetable sculpture which also has many uses. The 'uncurled' grain of the vegetable retains its tension, so whatever you cut from your sheet of vegetable will 'spring back' into curls.

Twists (*yori-udo*): Cut your sheet on the diagonal at 1½in intervals. The strips will pop into corkscrews.

Thunderclouds (*kaminari*): Roll a vegetable sheet back up again — as tightly as you can without splitting it — and slice as thinly as you can crosswise. The fine curly filaments that result are a standard 'bed' for *sashimi* (raw fish).

Fan (*ohgi-giri*): Vegetables such as cucumber, carrot and eggplant can all be made into handsome 'fans'.

Decorative citrus peel: This is a clever way to treat the citrus peel that lends its color and savor to soups. Start with a little oblong section of peel, trimmed to a square. Make one cut in each direction, to within ¼in of the end. A little 'Z' will result. Twist and tuck.

Mountain Shape (*yama-gata*) or **Alternate Cut** (*kiri-chigai*): Japanese cucumbers or asparagus tips can be used for this cut. By making an alternate, diagonal cut either side of the vegetable (do not cut through to the other side) you will produce a little 'mountain' for garnishing.

CUTTING A FLOWER SHAPE

The flower cut (*hana-giri*): This is one of the most popular Japanese decorative cuts, although it is also one of the more complicated ones to do. Choose large carrots, *daikon*, or any other long and solid vegetable. When the cut has been made, the shape should resemble a cherry blossom flower. You need steady fingers and a sharp knife to do this cut successfully. Alternatively, you can buy a *hana-giri* cutter from a Japanese goods store.

1. Cut a carrot or daikon into pieces 2in long. Make 5 slits lengthwise, about ¼in deep. Slits should be evenly spaced.

2. Halfway between 2 slits peel round with a sharp knife toward the bottom of the slit, making the corner smooth and round. Repeat.

3. Slice the vegetable to the thickness required. It is advisable to use thin slices for garnishes and thick ones for simmered dishes.

4. Alternatively, use a hana-gari cutter. They are widely used, even by chefs. The vegetable should be sliced first into ½in thick pieces.

COOKING TECHNIQUES

Cooking, like seasoning, is never overdone. In many ways, cooking is merely a kind of extension of seasoning — heat is used to seal certain good tastes into the fresh ingredients, or, as in the simple process called salt-broiling, to bring out the natural deliciousness of, say, the fish or chicken.

Broiling: Next to the art of cutting and serving raw fish, this is probably the most straight-forward category in Japanese cuisine. Broiling (*yakimono*) primarily means exposing fish or chicken and certain vegetables, along with the occasional beef, pork, or venison, to high heat from a charcoal fire. Densely forested Japan has produced fine charcoal since time immemorial, and charcoal-burning has long been a sideline for struggling farmers in the Japanese hinterland. It is fitting that water and charcoal, two of the few real resources that Japan possesses, should provide the basis for so much good eating.

The Japanese broil food under extreme heat in order to seal the outside of food and preserve the tender moistness inside the fish and chicken morsels. They broil with skewers almost exclusively too, since skewering supports and maintains the original shape of the ingredient better than rack or net broiling. You need not be a purist here, however; the sorts of charcoal broilers available in the West will do to make many dishes, and using the broiler in your oven is also a passable substitute. Still, there is nothing more delicious than a piping-hot salt-broiled small fish just off the fire, and given the availability of small Japanese broilers (*hibachi*)

abroad, there is no reason why you should not treat yourself to the real experience. If you do not have a *hibachi*, any arrangement that you can fix up to securely support skewers over a charcoal fire will do perfectly well.

The Japanese use smokeless charcoal. The 'smoky' quality of barbecue is not the point — the point is *heat*, heat that sears and protects taste.

The *yakimono* category is a bit broader than broiling per se — the use of a pan is also defined by the verb *yaki*. It therefore includes pan-fried dishes like the Japanese omelet and modern dishes such as *sukiyaki* (which is a hybrid in that it is a *nabemono* made up of pan-fried — or pot-fried — ingredients).

Steaming: Steamed foods (or *mushimono*) do not make up a large category, but steaming as a method is very respectful of the values of Japanese cuisine. Steam maintains texture, enhances color, and cooks quickly. When you steam Japanese-style, remember that the one indispensable piece of equipment is a steaming platform that is flat. Many dishes require that several ingredients be steamed together on a plate but commercial 'folding' steaming platforms, because of their shape and the handle in the middle, make it quite

impossible to balance a plate there for this purpose. However, these platforms are fine for single ingredients, like a bunch of spinach.

Simmering: The largest category of Japanese dishes is *nimono* (simmered things). Under this capacious heading fall not only delicate, bite-sized pieces of fish served with a simple garnish, but also the great, bubbling stews that play an important part in rural and regional cuisine.

Dashi stock, sweet *sake* (*mirin*), *sake*, soysauce and *miso*, in one combination or another, make up almost all the simmering stocks that the Japanese use, although there are endless subtle variations. *Sake* is particularly important as a tenderizer for fish, and soysauce is perhaps the most significant flavor-giver.

The main rule of simmering is not to do it to excess. Simmering medium and time are carefully adjusted for the ingredient in question, and no ingredient is allowed to lose its natural texture. Many simmering techniques are merely means of imparting a subtle *dashi* or soy flavour to a vegetable. Boiling before-hand, which is done in many cases, is a means of sealing in color and fresh taste, and it stands to reason that the subsequent simmering should not undo this effort.

The Japanese utensil used for simmering, the 'drop-lid' or *otoshi-buta* (see page 18), ensures that the simmered food is completely penetrated by the stock, and cooks gently and evenly.

One-Pot Cooking: This category includes popular familiars like *sukiyaki* and *shabu shabu* and the thick, hearty, and none-too-subtle winter-time stews from the north of Japan. With this technique, ingredients are pre-cut into bite-sized pieces and cooked at the table. One-pots (*nabemono*) are among the most enjoyable of Japanese eating experiences: the conviviality, sense of sharing, and party-humour that the

Japanese love so well are at their height when friends gather to dip their chopsticks in a common pot, toss off a few pots of *sake*, and laugh at the blustery winds.

Deep-Frying: Nothing shows the good taste and ingenuity of traditional Japanese cooks better than the way they have made deep-frying, a thoroughly foreign technique, into one of the wonders of the Japanese kitchen. By Japanizing it — in other words making it simple, subtle, and technically perfect — they have naturalized a technique that came to Japan from both Europe and China. The port city of Nagasaki already had a rich Chinese heritage by the sixteenth

century, when southern Europeans arrived as missionaries and traders. To Chinese styles of frying were added the Spanish and Portuguese love of fried seafood, and *agemono* was born. *Tempura* is the most famous of these early dishes with a foreign flavor, and it is certainly the glory of this style. I once had a fascinating lesson in cross-cultural eating in a Japanese restaurant in Mexico. I ordered *tempura*, curious to see how it would come out in a Latin country. The restaurant was in the city of Guadalajara,

The one-pot dish sukiyaki is in the process of being cooked, with paper-thin beef, 'flower-cut' vegetables and Chinese cabbage already sizzling in the pan.

and the cuisine of this region makes good use of fresh shellfish and other seafood. Accordingly, the shrimp in the *tempura* was deliciously fresh. However, the part of the dish that intrigued me most was the coat of batter that covered the shrimp — this was dense, delicious and deeply-golden. The dish had, as it were, returned to its origins in southern Europe.

Japanese *tempura*, of course, is different. In Tokyo it is golden in color, and in Ōsaka it is snowy white, but in both cities and everywhere else in Japan, it is divinely light. The batter is not really something which covers and transforms the fish, shellfish or vegetable — it just whispers around it, adding an additional taste and texture — another case of Japanese cooking as an extension of Japanese seasoning.

A few simple tips on making good *tempura* will be found in the recipe on page 138; in this section I shall simply note three rules for *agemono* in general. The oil used is clear and nearly tasteless. Japanese cooks rarely use butter or other animal fats (there are some delicious exceptions — buttered Indian corn in Hokkaidō, for example). Safflower, corn, and even peanut oil are all fine for Japanese deep-frying, but highly-flavored vegetable oils should always be avoided. Try blending oils until you get exactly the color and texture you want.

Japanese fried food is never

greasy. This is accomplished by keeping the oil at a high, even temperature so that an intense heat seals the outside immediately, and then cooks the inside by radiation. The principle here is plainly derived from charcoal broiling.

Food is served immediately after it comes out of the oil and is briefly drained. The limitation of space that every Japanese urbanite has to put up with is actually a blessing when it comes to food. The tiny one-counter, 10-seat food stalls and mini-restaurants throughout Japan's cities often specialize in a single dish, and the food is always piping hot and freshly cooked, as it is prepared right in front of the customer's eyes; these factors combine to make these little

Shrimp are being deep-fried in hot oil, having previously been dipped into batter. The result — crispy, light tempura.

places even better at what they do than an expensive, exclusive restuarant.

If your kitchen is similarly cramped, it need not be a problem. When you cook at home you can deliver food to your guests with as much despatch as any *tempura* cook in Ōsaka. Of course, all side dishes in an *agemono* meal should be prepared well beforehand so the cook can concentrate on frying and serving. I think you will agree that the pleasure you can give your guests this way more than makes up for your having to be the last one to sit and eat.

BEVERAGES

*T*he Japanese drink four beverages with native cuisine: *sake*, beer, whiskey and tea. There are no secret, special regional drinks, but there are excellent local varieties of tea and *sake*. Beer and whiskey, imported drinks at first, are now produced by a very small number of national concerns, and do as much to unify the nation's taste as television.

Sake: Many myths and stories surround Japan's incomparable alcoholic beverage — *sake* — the drink of the Shintō gods, of Emperors, shōguns, poets and philosophers. Probably Japan's oldest drink, this water-clear, fragrant essence of boiled rice is not a wine. Whereas wine is fermented by the natural must that grows on grapes, *sake* is first boiled, then yeast is added to begin the alcohol-making process; this makes it a sort of beer. But *sake* does not effervesce; it just sits quietly, limpid, in the cup, waiting to accompany the subtle tastes of a Japanese meal.

Foreign visitors to Japanese restaurants are most familiar with warm *sake*, but the Japanese enjoy it all the year round in many different ways. Heated *sake* goes naturally with chilly weather; it is also fine drunk at room temperature and, in the muggy depths of summer, the Japanese drink it chilled from square cups, originally used as merchants' measures. It is the most convivial of drinks, and devotees insist that a *sake*

hangover is mild compared with other types. *Sake* is heated in small bottles known as *tokkuri* or *chōshi*; these are immersed in a pan of water and the water is brought to the boil. Care has to be taken not to overheat the *sake*, however, as this would naturally blunt the taste a bit. A good temperature for serving *sake* is about 106-108°F.

Beer: The first beer brewed in Japan — in the 1870s — was for the consumption of foreigners in Yokohama's European settlement. The Japanese

government soon became involved in its production, sponsoring the development of barley and hops in newly-reclaimed lands in Hokkaidō. By the turn of the century, urban Japanese were enjoying beer in beer halls based on the European and American models. The foreign brew remained a sign of city sophistication, however, until the post-World War II era, when it spread throughout the country. In the 1960s, it surpassed *sake* in figures for total consumption. Today, beer, particularly lager, is every

A selection of Japanese drinks and drinking vessels: *1. Sake 2. Beer 3. Melon liqueur 4. 'Everyday' Japanese whiskey 5. Japanese whiskey for special occasions 6. Tokkuri (flask used for warming sake) 7 & 8. Sake cups 9. Masu (wooden rice measuring cup, used for drinking draft sake)*

A selection of teas: *1. Genmai-cha 2. Mugi-cha 3. Sencha 4. Hōji-cha*

bit as 'Japanese' as *tempura*.

Whiskey: Japan makes some fine blended whiskies, and an increasing number of people are ordering this drink, even in very traditional restaurants. Like Japanese beer, whiskey is mild and smooth; it is a bad idea to 'bruise' the palate when Japanese food is served. As with beer, whiskey best complements strong-flavored dishes like broiled meats and fish.

Tea: In Japan, tea is served at the end of a meal. The final course of a formal meal is rice, pickles and tea. I have always felt that there is something rather poetic in this, since this trio is also the typical frugal meal of people without great wealth, and it serves to remind well-heeled diners just how

simple Japanese eating can be. If you can love this combination of crisp, subtly pungent *takuan* or *senmai-zuke* pickles, filling and soothing white rice, and the rich but restraining flavor of fine green tea, you are truly on your way to becoming a Japanese epicure.

Tea spread firstly from China into the rest of Asia, and then throughout the world. Tea was known in Japan by around the eighth century; it was originally a medicinal plant and a stimulant, used to keep meditating monks and sutra-copying scholars awake. The second great age of tea in Japan began in the twelfth century and coincided with the strong influence of Zen Buddhism. Tea drinking became closely connected with the precepts of Zen, and its use

was confined mainly to the priesthood and aristocracy. In the sixteenth century, ordinary leaf tea became popular for all classes, and tea-drinking lost its aristocratic tone.

All Japanese tea is 'green', which means that it is steamed right after picking, a process that inhibits the enzyme changes that turn green tea into the 'black' variety. *Bancha*, the most common sort of leaf tea, is an all-purpose warmer-upper and thirst-quencher for the Japanese — the kind of tea that is served in big mugs in ordinary restaurants.

Sencha, a higher-grade leaf variety, is richer in color than *bancha*. It is not used as a thirst-quencher, and is drunk in small quantities, served in *sushi* shops or offered to special guests. *Gyokuro* of 'jewel-dew' is fine tea, the leaf version of the powdered tea used in the tea ceremony. Tea-ceremony tea, or *matcha*, is an emerald-green, frothy tea that is prepared by whipping powder in hot (*not* boiling) water. Good *matcha* is brilliantly green and slightly bitter. Other tea varieties include: *hōji-cha*; lightly roasted *bancha*; *genmai-cha*: *bancha* with little kernals of popped rice added; and *mugi-cha*: not in fact tea, despite having the suffix *cha* (tea) attached to its name, but barley water, which is usually served chilled.

COOKING AT HOME

*P*resentation is essential, even at the simplest Japanese meal. The Japanese do not serve large portions of any one dish. They place their foods in separate little bowls and dishes, and they are always careful to make the receptacles they use harmonize with the foods they place in them. A great variety of dishes and bowls, rather than a homogeneous set is used in a Japanese meal, and so the cook has a large amount of freedom to decide on the 'look' of each edible composition.

AT HOME, the Japanese have always eaten simply and 'simultaneously', crowding the table with soup, rice, pickles, tea and a titbit of simmered or broiled fish, subtracting or adding dishes depending upon the occasion. Except in a frugal Japanese meal, there are always several courses, and everything is usually laid out on the table at once, creating an impressive and mouthwatering spectacle.

There are three dishes in Japanese cookery that form a part of nearly every Japanese meal: rice, pickles (*tsukemono*) and soup (clear or *misoshiru*). Not only are they the standard fare for a frugal meal, they also make up the final part of a formal banquet. If a meal comprises more than this traditional trio, then the various cooking techniques are represented in the additional dishes — a broiled and simmered dish, for example, or a steamed and simmered dish.

The menus opposite have been composed from the recipes in the book. They illustrate some of the essential features of a Japanese meal: the balance of textures, flavors and colors, the range and variety of dishes, the uses of different cooking techniques, and the importance of rice, pickles and tea. They have been included to show the traditional ways that dishes are combined together and the number of dishes that the Japanese usually prepare for different types of meals at home.

The cook who takes on the challenge of preparing Japanese food must have a general knowledge of the standard cooking techniques. So, the recipes in the first section have been selected in order to present the basic tastes and techniques of Japanese cooking wherever it is done.

If you try these dishes, or merely read through them on your way to the regional specialties, you will note the constants in Japanese cuisine: the oft-repeated seasonings (soy, *sake*, fish stock), the simple but subtle techniques (swift boiling, cutting into small sections), and the pronounced 'family resemblances' among diverse dishes (some soups, for example, are simply simmered dishes with more hot liquid). Once you are aware of some of these things, the regional variations, which are sometimes as subtle as the addition of a single ingredient, will take on color in your mind and on your tongue.

The meal (*right*) *is a typical informal supper for one. The three essential dishes — rice, pickles and soup — are supplemented by a broiled dish and simmered dish 1. Rice 2. Miso soup 3. Yakimono — broiled cod fillet with ao-nori (green nori), dried nori seaweed flakes and chestnuts. 4. Nimono — simmered abura-age (deep-fried tōfu bag), stuffed with chicken and vegetables, garnished with snow peas 5. Tsukemono (pickles) — pickled Chinese cabbage, daikon, eggplant and konbu shreds.*

Breakfast

DASHIMAKI TAMAGO
(egg roll with grated daikon and soysauce)

TSUKEMONO
(pickled vegetables)

PLAIN BOILED RICE

MISO SOUP
(soup with tōfu cubes and finely chopped green onion)

JAPANESE GREEN TEA

Lunch

TENDON
(tempura on rice)

OR

TORI GOHAN
(chicken and rice)

CHAWAN MUSHI
(steamed custard and vegetables)

TSUKEMONO
(pickled vegetables)

FRESH FRUIT

Dinner

TROUT SHIOYAKI
(salted and broiled trout, garnished with vinegared ginger)

UMANI
(simmered chicken, daikon, carrots and bamboo shoots)

HŌRENSŌ NO GOMA-AE
(spinach tossed in sesame seed dressing)

PLAIN BOILED RICE

SUMASHI-JIRU
(clear soup with shrimp and vegetables)

FRESH FRUIT

JAPANESE GREEN TEA

Supper

SASHIMI
(prepared raw fish — lemon sole, tuna, salmon and squid garnished with daikon filaments served with wasabi and soysauce)

SUKIYAKI
(beef one-pot with vegetables cooked on the table, served with raw egg)

KYŪRI TO WAKAME NO SUNOMONO
(cucumber and seaweed salad in a vinegar dressing)

PLAIN BOILED RICE

FRESH FRUIT

JAPANESE GREEN TEA

基本料理

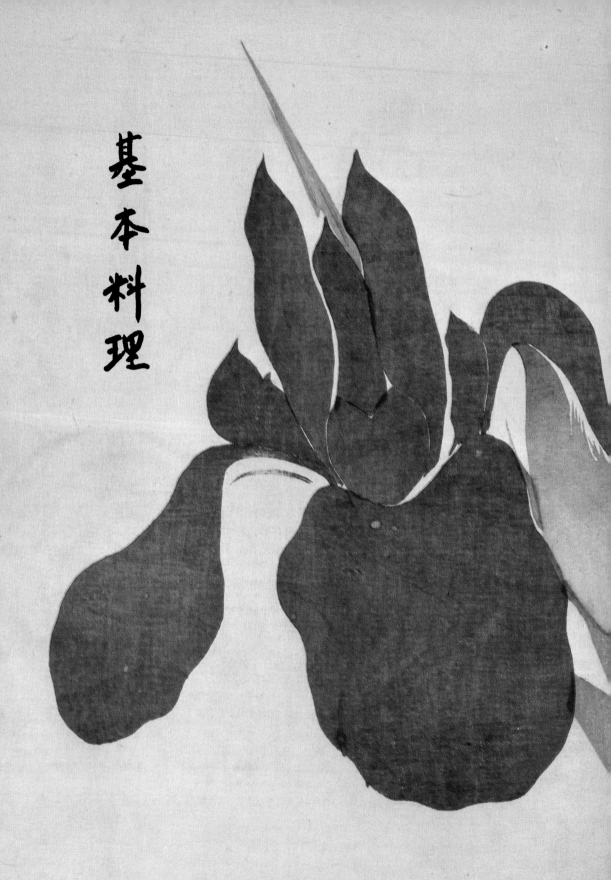

BASIC DISHES

SOUPS (Owanmono)

Soups play an essential role in Japanese cuisine and all the soups in this section are very familiar to every Japanese. The selection includes *miso* soup, a favorite at breakfast-time; clear soup, typically Japanese in its simplicity and subtlety of flavor, and *zōsui*, like the proverbial chicken soup, good for when you are ill.

Japanese soups are among the easiest dishes to adapt to a Western menu; indeed, French *nouvelle cuisine* sometimes includes clear Japanese soup, unaltered, in its sophisticated menus. For the purposes of home cooking, too, such ingenious and delicious dishes as *miso* soup are hard to improve upon.

The main thing to remember is that unlike many Japanese dishes, soups must be served steaming hot. Traditional style lacquer bowls with lids are perfect for retaining heat and with it, flavor.

SUMASHI-JIRU

(Clear Soup)

INGREDIENTS (Serves 6)
SUMASHI:
6 cups (48fl.oz) *ichiban*
    dashi
1¹/₂ tsp salt
¹/₂ tsp *soysauce*
1 tsp *sake*
salt

GARNISH:
¹/₂lb *plaice fillet (or any white*
    fish meat)
2 tbsp cornstarch
6 tightly curled mushrooms
1 stalk broccoli
2in section of *daikon*
citrus rind

(Illustration overleaf)

澄
汁

THIS IS A RECIPE for a delicious clear soup incorporating white fish and a variety of vegetables.

Preparation

Bring the *ichiban dashi* to a light simmer, and continue to simmer over a moderate heat for a few seconds. Then reduce the heat to low. Stir in the salt, soysauce, and *sake*. Sprinkle more salt to taste.

Cut the plaice fillet into six pieces and lightly season with salt and pepper. Roll the fish pieces in cornstarch and shake off excess. Wash the mushrooms in lightly salted water and pat dry. Roll the mushrooms in cornstarch.

Bring 2 cups (³/₄pt) of water to the boil in a saucepan and add the mushrooms. Cook for 3 minutes and take the mushrooms out of the saucepan. In the same boiling water add the fish fillets and simmer for 3 minutes or until the fillets are cooked. Drain.

Wash the broccoli and divide into thin sections to make six bunches. In salted water, cook the broccoli for a few minutes until the broccoli is just soft but still crunchy.

Skin the *daikon* and, using a very sharp knife, peel it very thinly in one piece all the way round (see page 34). Cut the thin *daikon* sheet diagonally into six.

Place one fish fillet, one broccoli stalk and one mushroom in each soup bowl. Pour hot *sumashi* soup over the ingredients. Serve garnished with *daikon* and citrus rind.

OZŌNI

(Soup with Rice Cake)

THIS IS A CELEBRATORY DISH, particularly favored at the joyous New Year holiday. There are many variations of *ozōni*, but the basic meaning of the term is a hearty soup that includes *mochi* rice cake. *Mochi* is a hearty, sticky 'taffy' that has a magical history in folklore. An ancient archer once used *mochi* cakes for target practice, and each time he scored a hit, the *mochi* cake turned into a beautiful white bird. Non-flying varieties of *mochi* may be purchased in Japanese food shops. The cakes should be soft, but if the ones you buy seem a little dry and hard, soak them in cold water for a couple of hours before use.

Preparation

Slice the chicken into thin strips, and sprinkle the strips with salt. Lightly salt a small amount of water, bring to the boil, and blanch the chicken until light white – about 1½ minutes. Drain.

Shuck and devein the shrimp, being careful to keep the tails intact. Boil the shrimp for about 2 minutes, or until blushed pink and firm. Place into chilled water to arrest cooking and set aside.

Cut the *daikon* into a hexagon shape (this shape recalls the felicitous Japanese tortoise) and slice into ¼in thick sections. Boil in lightly salted water for about 15 minutes, but be careful not to let the *daikon* sections get too soft. Drain and set aside.

Peel and wash the carrot and slice into small rounds (¼in). Boil in lightly salted water for about 10 minutes. Drain and set aside.

Boil the greens in lightly salted water until wilted and tender. Rinse under cold running water, squeeze out the moisture and pat dry with paper towelling. Chop coarsely and divide into four portions.

Cook the *mochi* cakes over charcoal or under a broiler. The surface should become golden-brown. Be careful not to burn the *mochi* surface anywhere. Turn to brown both sides.

Bring the *dashi* to a low boil in a large saucepan. Lower the heat to bring the *dashi* to a simmer, and add the soysauce and salt.

Place the *mochi* cakes in individual bowls; add the other ingredients – the chicken, shrimp, *daikon* hexagon, chrysanthemum portions and carrot rounds – to each bowl, making a pleasing arrangement. Then carefully pour in the soup, taking care not to disturb the arrangement. Eat while very hot.

INGREDIENTS (Serves 4)
½lb boned chicken, leg and
   breast, with skin
4 medium shrimp
2in wide section of *daikon*
   (white Japanese radish)
1 medium-sized carrot
8 sprigs edible
   chrysanthemum leaves
   (*shungiku*)
4 mochi cakes
3⅓ cups (27fl.oz) *ichiban
   dashi*
½ tsp salt
½ tsp soysauce

■ SUMASHI-JIRU (page 46)
Clear soup
Garnishes: *daikon and citrus rind*

■ MISO-SHIRU (page 50)
Clear soup, flavored with *miso*

HAMAGURI USHIO-JIRU

(Clam Consommé)

INGREDIENTS (Serves 6)
6 big clams
3in square of konbu, washed
    under cold running water
2 tsp soysauce
pinch of salt
2 tbsp sake
small bunch of trefoil, washed
    and trimmed
2in section of daikon peeled
    and cut into thin strips

(Illustration overleaf)

HERE IS ANOTHER VARIETY of clear soup. Clams are a very popular inclusion.

Preparation

To remove sand from the clams, soak them in slightly salted water and keep in a dark place.

Combine 6 cups (2¼ pints) of cold water, the konbu square and clams in a large saucepan. Bring to a high boil, then remove the konbu and discard. Continue to boil for approximately 2 minutes, or until the clams open. Skim off any residue that floats to the top. Take off the heat. Remove the clams and separate the clam meat from the shell, replacing one piece of meat in each shell so that everybody receives one shell each. (You only need six shells.) Place one clam in each bowl.

Carefully pour the soup in which the clams were cooked into another saucepan so as to separate out the sand floating at the bottom of the soup. Put the soup back on the heat and season with salt and soysauce. When boiling add the sake and trefoil. Boil for 30 seconds and pour over the clam in each bowl. Garnish with daikon strips and serve hot.

MISO-SHIRU

(Miso Soup)

INGREDIENTS (Serves 4)
½ cake tōfu
4 tbsp red miso
3½ cups (28fl.oz) ichiban
    dashi or niban dashi
4 tbsp finely chopped green
    onion
sansho pepper

(Illustration previous page)

THERE ARE THOUSANDS of variations of this hearty soup. Use your ingenuity; it is actually very difficult to make a miso soup that does not taste good.

Preparation

Drain the tōfu. Prepare the miso — it must be slightly diluted with 2 tbsp of stock and blended thoroughly before it is put into the stock pot. This assures that the miso will blend smoothly with the dashi stock.

Spoon the miso into the stock a little at a time, blending carefully. Simmer over a medium heat. When all the miso is dissolved in the stock, add the tōfu. The Japanese like very small (½in) tōfu cubes in their miso soups, but larger ones give the soup a heartier look. Keep the soup simmering in order to heat the tōfu, but do not allow the soup to boil — you are not actually cooking the tōfu.

Ladle into individual bowls, filling them about two-thirds of the way to the top. Japanese-style lacquer bowls with tops are by far the best, but narrow deep bowls of any sort will do. The flat, wide

Western soup bowl is not a good idea as the soup will lose too much heat.

Garnish each bowl with finely chopped green onion and add a little bit of *sansho* pepper; serve immediately, as with all Japanese soups.

ZŌSUI

(Rice Broth)

ANY JAPANESE will tell you that this warming, easy-to-eat soup is just right for the times when you are ill or out of sorts. As its name implies, *Zōsui* ('miscellany soup') is also one of those valuable dishes that help you put leftovers to good use.

Preparation

Heat the *dashi* in a saucepan, and add the salt and soysauce. Do not let this broth boil. Set aside when heated through. Prepare the chicken; if you are using cooked leftover chicken, simply shred it into fine strips and add to the soup. With uncooked chicken, bone and skin the breast and cut the chicken into thin strips. Blanch the chicken in a small amount of water until light white — about 40 seconds. Drain the chicken and add to the soup.

Slice the shiitake mushrooms into thin strips and add to the soup. Simmer the mixture for 10 minutes, stirring occasionally.

Rinse the rice in cold water; drain. Add the rice to the soup and stir until the rice is smoothly distributed.

Bring 2 cups (³/₄pt) salted water to the boil, and blanch the greens for a few seconds, until the leaves are slightly wilted. Drain, and pat dry with paper towelling. Chop the leaves coarsely and add to the soup.

Bring the soup to the boil and stir, using a chopstick. Pour the beaten egg into the soup, and continue to stir. Cover the saucepan for 30 seconds or so to allow the egg to cook briefly. Add the ginger juice, stir, and serve very hot. The Japanese like to eat *zōsui* with a couple of tart pickled plums (*ume-boshi*).

INGREDIENTS (Serves 4)

3 cups (24fl.oz) ichiban dashi or niban dashi

¹/₄ tsp salt

¹/₂ tsp soysauce

1 chicken breast (leftovers will be fine, as long as the chicken was cooked simply — broiled or steamed)

2 small, dried shiitake mushrooms (soften them in water for about 30 minutes before use)

1¹/₂-2 cups (9-12oz) cooked rice (for instructions on cooking rice, see page 94; leftover rice is often used)

4 green leaves (spinach or chrysanthemum)

1 beaten egg

1¹/₂ tsp ginger juice, squeezed from grated fresh ginger

(Illustration overleaf)

■ HAMAGURI USHIO-JIRU (page 50)
Clam soup
Garnish: *daikon* strips

■ <u>ZŌSUI</u> (page 51)
Rice broth

SLICED RAW FISH (Sashimi)

*R*aw fish, which sounds like a rather bizarre delicacy to many foreigners, is really the heart of Japanese cuisine. Fresh, glowing fish, scaled, skinned, and sliced into oblongs and squares, is the height of perfection for nearly all of the 100 million seafood-lovers who live in Japan.

It is very hard indeed not to enjoy well-prepared *sashimi*. The 'fishy' smell that puts some people off is washed away with lots of cold water. The flesh of many fish is as tender as cool butter and the taste, although quite unique, is startlingly delicious. Nutritionally, *sashimi* is also extremely healthy: rich in protein and iron — a 'health food' that is, for a change, highly enjoyable.

The preparation of raw fish is such a speciality that most Japanese get their sashimi from restaurants. Still, one can manage reasonable sashimi at home — as long as the freshest fish is used. If you live inland and do not have access to really fresh saltwater fish, then use the freshwater variety. Prepared with the correct dipping sauce, there is hardly a single fish or shellfish in the ocean or the lakes that cannot be made into sashimi.

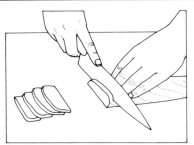

Tuna: *This is sold filleted and in lengths of sashimi thickness. So simply buy the length you need and cut into slices ¹⁄₂in thick.*

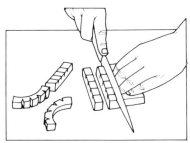

Squid: *Make little slits lengthwise on the top of the squid. They make the squid less chewy. Then cut crosswise into slices ¹⁄₄in thick.*

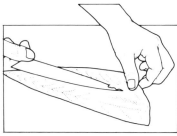

Sea bass: *1. After filleting, remove any remaining bones with a knife. Also use a tweezer to take out the hidden bones in the centre.*

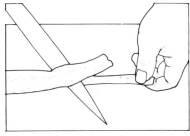

2. Cut the fillet in half. Separate the skin and the flesh at the tail end and, holding the skin in one hand, slide the knife down in the other hand.

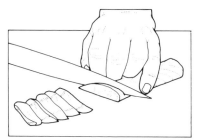

3. Cut the fillet on a slight diagonal into slices ¹⁄₄-¹⁄₂in thick, using a very sharp knife.

Carp: *1. Place your fingers on the fish and, with the bevelled edge of the knife almost horizontal, cut off paper-thin slices.*

2. Remove the paper-thin slices carefully, one by one. This method is most appropriate for firm, white-fleshed fish.

3. Transfer the slices carefully to a platter and arrange them in a rosette pattern. Add garnishes of your choice and serve immediately.

SASHIMI

(Raw, Sliced Fish)

THE MOST IMPORTANT part of preparing sliced, raw fish is to ensure that the fish is absolutely fresh. Frozen fish must not be used. A wide variety of fish can be used for *sashimi* and either a single kind of fish, or a mixture can be served.

Preparation

Clean the fish carefully, then fillet it, using the *sanmai-oroshi* technique (for cleaning and filleting instructions, see pages 29-31). There are various methods for cutting *sashimi* — the cut you choose should depend on the type of fish you are using (see opposite).

Having cut your fish, arrange the slices attractively. The presentation of *sashimi* is very important. Serving plates and garnishes should be chosen with care to complement the color and shape of the fish. You can either serve *sashimi* on one plate — slices look very attractive arranged in a rosette pattern, resting on a bed of shred-cut *daikon*, or on individual plates. Use garnishes of your choice, such as a curl of carrot, a decorative leaf, or mounds of finely chopped green onion.

Give each person a dab of *wasabi* paste and a bowl of dipping sauce. Each person mixes the *wasabi* paste with the dipping sauce and dips the fish into the sauce before eating.

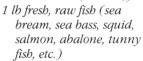

INGREDIENTS (Serves 4)
1 lb fresh, raw fish (sea bream, sea bass, squid, salmon, abalone, tunny fish, etc.)
½ lb daikon (shred-cut)
2 tbsp wasabi powder, mixed with water to make a thick paste
3 to 5 tbsp soysauce, or tosa joyu (see below)

(Illustration overleaf)

TOSA-JŌYU

(Shikoku Soysauce)

TOSA IS THE ANCIENT NAME for the southern portion of the island of Shikoku — famous for its bonito catch. This rich and complex soy-based dipping sauce is a popular Tosa product that all of Japan enjoys with *sashimi* (sliced raw fish). Flaked bonito gives it its savor.

Preparation

Mix the *sake* and *mirin* together in a small saucepan and heat gently, until there is a pronounced aroma. Light the fumes with a kitchen match and burn off the alcohol, gently agitating the pan.

Wipe the *konbu* with a damp cloth to help release the flavor. Combine all the ingredients and let them stand in a cool place for 24 hours.

Then strain the sauce through a cheesecloth into a jar, seal, and keep in a cool, dark place. *Tosa-jōyu* takes 30 days to mature properly, and it is at its best for one year thereafter.

INGREDIENTS
Makes 1 cup (8fl.oz)
5 tsp sake
3 tbsp mirin
1 square konbu (kelp), about 2in square
3 tbsp tamari sauce
1 cup (8fl.oz) dark soysauce
1 handful dried bonito flakes (hana-katsuo)

■ SASHIMI (page 54)
A selection of sliced raw fish and shellfish
Garnishes: _shiso leaves and buds_, _wasabi horseradish_,
wakame seaweed and decoratively cut carrot

■ TROUT SASHIMI (page 55)
Garnishes: *chopped green onion and momiji-oroshi*

BROILING AND PAN-FRYING
(Yakimono)

While charcoal cooking is a technique for parties, outdoor barbecues and other special occasions in the West, it is an everyday style in Japan. Even in the smallest flats, the Japanese mount skewer racks over gas flames, trying to approximate the charcoal effect, and broil away in spite of smoke, spatter and smell. If you intend to explore Japanese cuisine at all, you should familiarize yourself with this simple and delicious way of sealing in and bringing out natural flavors in fish, meat and vegetables.

Broiling is usually done by placing food on skewers on a grill over a charcoal fire. Skewering performs two important functions: it helps to preserve and maintain the original shape of the ingredient during cooking and to ensure efficient cooking. The Japanese have invented a variety of ways of skewering food, and this popular method is used not only for fish, but also for a wide range of other ingredients.

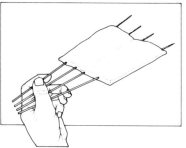

Tate-gushi (*'lengthwise skewering'*): *Insert skewers lengthwise along the grain of the fish.*

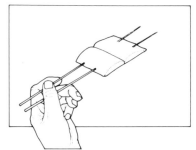

Hira-gushi (*'flat skewering'*): *Insert skewers crosswise into the middle of the fish. Suitable for fillets.*

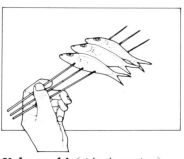

Yoko gushi (*side skewering*): *1. Place 2 to 3 fish on a board, lined horizontally and insert 3 to 4 long metal skewers*

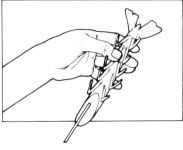

Prawn skewering: *1. Keeping the prawn straight, poke a skewer lengthwise through the underside of the prawn.*

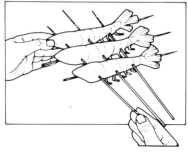

2. Insert 2 to 3 skewers crosswise. Insert the 2 outer skewers on a diagonal so that they meet and can be gripped easily.

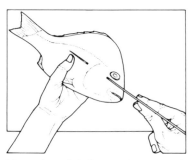

Unergi-gushi (*'wave skewering'*): *1. Insert a skewer just behind the eye area. Bring the skewer out further down the fish on the same side.*

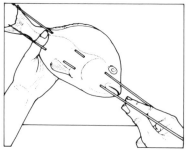

2. Bend the fish slightly and insert the skewer closer to the tail. Bring it out again at the base of the tail.

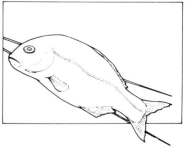

3. Be careful never to poke the skewers through to the other side of the fish so you have a 'good' side to present to your guests.

AJI SHIOYAKI

(Salt-Broiling)

WHEN THE JAPANESE broil a whole fish by this or any other method, they call the result *sugata-yaki* ('form-broiling') because the form of the fish is preserved whole and intact. Salt-broiling is a simple, ancient method that works by a natural logic. The salting acts to bring delicious fats and oils to the surface of the fish, enhancing its taste so much that it is as if delicious sauces have been added. But nothing is added, outside of a simple squeeze of lemon when it is time to eat the fish. The ubiquitous soysauce, of course, should also be available for dipping.

INGREDIENTS (Serves 4)
4 horse mackerel (aji), fresh trout or other medium-sized fish, scaled and cleaned (see page 30), with head and tail intact
salt
lemon wedges
soysauce

(Illustration overleaf)

Preparation

Skewering: Although you can salt-broil using any type of broiler, you will produce the best flavor by skewer-broiling over charcoal. There are various fish-skewering techniques. The one used here is *uneri-gushi* which means 'twisting on the skewer'; a fish skewered in this way looks as if it is swimming bravely upstream.

Place the fish in front of you, its belly toward you and its head pointed to the right. This is the 'wrong side' of the fish, the side you will place down on the plate when you serve your guest. First, eviscerate the fish (see page 30). Insert the skewer just behind the eye area. Push it into the fish, taking care that the skewer does not poke through the other, or 'right' side. Bring the skewer back through and out about 1½in from where it first went in. Bend the fish slightly and insert the skewer closer to the tail. As before, push the skewer in but do not poke it all the way through; instead, bring it out again on the 'wrong' side at the very base of the tail.

The fish and skewer combination will have to sit securely while broiling, so you should parallel your first skewer with another a short distance away.

Salting: Take a generous pinch of salt between your fingers and rub it gently into the tail and all the fins. Use as much salt as you need to make the fins stand up and to give them a generous coating. This is the 'cosmetic' salting, entirely for looks. Toasted salt in these places will form a snowy crust.

Lightly salt the entire fish; this is the 'flavor' salting.

Broiling and serving: Broil the 'good' side first. The heat must be high. When pinkish 'sweat' bubbles form on the upper surface of your fish, turn it and broil the 'wrong side'. Twist the skewers several times as you broil, but turn the fish itself only once, to minimize the loss of oils that give it such a delicious flavor.

Remove from the broiler and take out the skewers. Serve the fish 'good side up' with a simple garnish like a lemon wedge or pickled red ginger. Dip it in soysauce if you wish — but not before tasting salt-broiled fish all by itself!

■ <u>AJI SHIOYAKI</u> (page 59)
Salt-broiled horse mackerel
Garnishes: *pickled red ginger and snow peas*

EBI KUSHIYAKI

(Skewer-Broiled Shrimp)

INGREDIENTS (Serves 4)
12 large shrimp
2 tsp sake
1 tsp kosher salt
soysauce
lemon wedges

(Illustration overleaf)

海
老
串
焼
き

THE SHIOYAKI (salt-broiling) technique is adapted here to the delicate and subtle flavor of fresh shrimp. Again, *sake* appears as a tenderizer.

Preparation

Remove the whiskers and tip of the snout by cutting the shrimp's head off just before the eyes. Using long metal skewers, skewer each shrimp laterally. Then, taking three shrimp at a time, skewer them 'fanwise' (see page 58).

Sprinkle the shrimp lightly with *sake*, leave them to stand for a few minutes, sprinkle with salt and broil. You will only need to broil the first side for about 2 minutes, and the other side for a little more than 1 minute; remember that after foods are taken off the fire, retained heat goes on working for a short time.

Serve as a canapé, with soysauce for dipping. Add garnishes of your choice such as carrot slices, lemon wedges and decorative bamboo leaves.

DASHIMAKI TAMAGO

(Egg Roll)

INGREDIENTS (Serves 1)
3 eggs, well-beaten
1/3 cup (3fl.oz) ichiban dashi
  or niban dashi
1/4 tsp dark soysauce
pinch of salt
1 tbsp grated daikon (white
  radish)
soysauce
vegetable oil
1 sheet toasted nori seaweed,
  cut into fine shreds

(Illustration overleaf)

だ
し
巻
き
卵

THIS UNIQUE OMELET requires a certain amount of manual dexterity and the aid of the special oblong Japanese omelet pan (see page 20). Once you have mastered the technique, however, you will understand why Japanese in every region of the country are fond of this tiny, tidy egg roll.

Preparation

Mix together the beaten eggs, the *dashi*, 1/4 tsp soysauce, and the salt in a bowl. Stir well.

Moisten the grated *daikon* with a little soysauce, form it into a little clump and set aside; this will be the garnish for your completed omelet.

Lightly brush the bottom of your omelet pan with vegetable oil. Heat the oil over a moderately high heat. Test the temperature by scattering a couple of drops of water across the pan; if the water evaporates instantly, the oil is hot enough for sautéing.

Pour enough egg mixture into the skillet to coat the bottom lightly. Move the pan over the heat for about 10 seconds, or until the egg begins to set. Then, gently roll the omelet up, 2in at a time, until there is a 'roll' at the nearest end of the pan. (You may use a spatula to do this, but short chopsticks work even better, if you are comfortable using them (see page 18).

Brush more oil onto the skillet and slide the first complete roll to the far end of the pan. Pour another thin layer of egg into the pan, allowing this layer 10 seconds or so to 'set', as before. Make sure you allow some of the egg to run underneath the first roll.

Roll again, from the far end toward you, this time wrapping your first roll *inside* the second as you go.

Oil the skillet bottom, as before, slide the roll to the end, and pour another layer. Repeat until the egg mixture is used up.

When the roll is complete, lift it out with a spatula, and cut it in half crosswise. Garnish with soy-and-grated-*daikon* and fine shreds of toasted *nori* seaweed, and serve.

A variation on this dish is *sobe tamago yaki* (seashore rolled omelet), which takes its name, sensibly enough, from the sheet of dried laver seaweed (*nori*) that is added. Unfold a full sheet of the laver and divide the sheet into thirds. Freshen the flavor of the strips by passing one side over a flame. When you pour each new egg layer out, lay one of the *nori* sheets on it after it has 'set' and just before you begin to roll it. You will produce a roll with a spiral trace of dark green at the end.

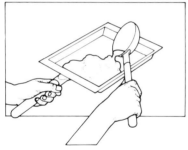

1. Having brushed the pan with vegetable oil, pour one-third of the egg mixture into a Japanese egg pan and tilt until the mixture spreads evenly.

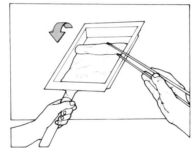

2. When the mixture begins to bubble around the edges, tilt the pan and, using chopsticks, roll the egg layer toward you.

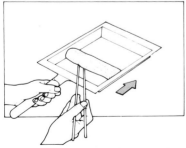

3. Push the roll to the far end of the pan. Moisten the pan with oil and add more egg mixture.

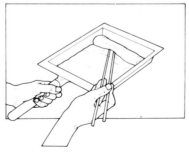

4. Lift the first roll to allow the new layer to spread beneath it. Roll again, wrapping your first roll in the new sheet.

■ DASHIMAKI TAMAGO (page 62)
Rolled egg
Garnishes: *shredded nori and grated daikon mixed with soysauce*

■ EBI KUSHIYAKI (page 62)
Skewer-broiled shrimp
Garnishes: *wakame seaweed, lemon slices, carrot pieces, decoratively cut cucumber, tsubu miso and miniature daikon*

YAKINASU

(Broiled Eggplant)

INGREDIENTS (Serves 4/5)
10 Japanese eggplants
vegetable oil
soysauce
1 tbsp ginger juice
1 tbsp grated fresh ginger

(Illustration overleaf)

焼
す
茄

THE JAPANESE EGGPLANT is a great deal smaller than the Western variety. Like its larger brother, it is a versatile vegetable, particularly delicious when broiled.

Preparation

Brush the eggplant lightly with vegetable oil and make a few small holes with a toothpick to allow the oil and heat to penetrate.

Broil over a very hot charcoal fire until the skin becomes quite dark. The skin will wrinkle and draw away slightly from the flesh on the inside. Turn frequently for even broiling. Broiling should take about 20 minutes, depending on the size of the eggplants and the intensity of the heat.

When ready, remove the eggplants from the broiler and immerse them immediately in cold water. When they are cool enough to handle easily, peel them and discard the skin.

Eggplants may be sliced or served whole. Place two on each person's plate and top with a little splash of soysauce and ginger juice. Garnish with more grated ginger, or a lemon wedge if desired.

TORINIKU NO SHIOYAKI

(Salt-Broiled Chicken)

INGREDIENTS (Serves 4))
4 boned chicken breast halves
2 tbsp sake
salt
lemon wedges

鶏
肉
塩
焼
き

SALT-BROILING IS a delicious way to prepare chicken; however care must be taken not to overcook the meat. Broiled chicken Japanese style should be moist all the way through and pink at the bone.

Preparation

Sprinkle the breasts with *sake* and leave them to stand for 5 to 10 minutes: *sake* acts as a fine chicken tenderizer.

You can skewer chicken breasts (or fish fillets) 'fanwise'. Insert three short skewers in such a way that they radiate out like a fan. This arrangement not only looks handsomely 'Japanese', it is also good for balancing the breasts securely.

Sprinkle the breasts liberally with salt on both sides. Broil the skin side first, until it is a golden color (about 7 minutes). Then turn the pieces and broil the other side for about 4 minutes.

This dish may be served hot, warm, or at room temperature. Salt-broiling preserves flavor whatever the temperature.

GYŪNIKU TERIYAKI

(Beef *Teriyaki*)

IN THE TECHNIQUE TERIYAKI a marinade of *sake*, *mirin* and soysauce is used to glaze the dish. In this recipe, the main ingredient is tender beef. Care must be taken not to overcook the meat.

牛
肉
照
焼

Preparation

Heat a skillet and add 2 tbsp oil. When the oil is hot, add the zucchini slices and sauté both sides until slightly brown. Remove the zucchini to a warm place and keep warm. In the skillet add another tbsp oil and sauté the mushrooms over a high heat. When the mushrooms are cooked and slightly brown, place them on a warm plate and keep warm. Add a further 1 or 2 tbsp oil and sauté the onion slices. When they are slightly brown, remove them from the pan and keep warm. Drain the oil then heat a further 3 tbsp oil. When the oil is very hot, quickly sauté the bean sprouts and set them aside on a warm plate. Keep all the sautéd vegetables warm while the beef steak is being cooked.

Lightly salt the steaks and leave for 5 to 10 minutes. In a skillet heat 2 tbsp oil and sauté the steaks over a high heat, one by one (add more oil if necessary), until both sides are brown. Pour 1 tbsp *sake* over each steak and cook for another 1 to 2 minutes covered with a lid. Remove the steaks to a warm plate. In the skillet, add the *mirin* and soysauce and mix with the meat juices (this makes the *teriyaki* sauce). Return the steaks to the pan and quickly coat with the *teriyaki* sauce (about 30 seconds each side).

Place one steak, a quarter of the bean sprouts, mushrooms and onion and zucchini slices on each of four plates. Pour the remaining *teriyaki* sauce in the pan over the steaks, and serve immediately.

INGREDIENTS (Serves 4)
vegetable oil
1 large zucchini, thinly sliced
¼ lb mushrooms, washed
    and halved if large
½ lb bean sprouts, washed
    and trimmed
4 sirloin steaks

FOR THE TERIYAKI SAUCE:
4 tbsp sake
3 tbsp mirin
3 tbsp dark soysauce

(Illustration overleaf)

■ GYŪNIKU TERIYAKI (page 67)
Broiled beef

■ <u>YAKINASU</u> (page 66)
Broiled eggplant
Garnish: *bonito flakes*

69

STEAMING (Mushimono)

Steamed dishes form a small, miscellaneous, but important category in Japanese cooking. While Western cooks regularly steam ingredients, chiefly vegetables, in Japanese cooking there are a number of complex and beautiful steamed dishes that require the assembly of many different ingredients on a steaming-rack.

Despite the great heat generated by the steaming process, many *mushimono* are allowed to cool before being served. Room-temperature side dishes may be somewhat difficult to adjust to at first, but Japanese culinary wisdom is not to be doubted: often, not even heat is allowed to intervene between the eater and the dish's natural flavor.

CHAWAN MUSHI

(Steamed Custard and Vegetables)

INGREDIENTS (Serves 4)
4 medium shrimp, peeled
  deveined and split in half
  lengthwise
salt
1/2 chicken breast, boned and
  cubed
few drops of *sake*
1/4 tsp soysauce
12 ginkgo nuts

CUSTARD:
4 eggs
2²/₃ cups (22fl.oz) ichiban
  dashi
1/2 tsp salt
1/8 tsp soysauce
4 tsp grated fresh ginger

(Illustrated overleaf)

THIS IS AN ALL-TIME NATIONAL FAVORITE, which is enjoyed informally by itself and as part of *haute cuisine*. Despite its name, it is not a sweet, eggy dessert, but a steamed-egg dish with traditional Japanese flavoring.

Preparation
Sprinkle the shrimp with a little salt. Sprinkle the chicken pieces with a little *sake* and allow them to stand for a moment; then sprinkle the chicken lightly with salt and soysauce. Place one shrimp, some chicken cubes, and three of the ginkgo nuts in each of four ramekin dishes or mugs.

Beat the eggs thoroughly and stir in the *dashi*, salt, and soysauce. Pour the mixture over the ingredients in the ramekins.

Cover the ramekins with aluminum foil and place them in a steamer. Bring the water to the boil, then partially cover the steamer and steam over a moderate heat for about 10 minutes. The custard should be firm on top. Because of the moisture given off by the various ingredients, *chawan mushi* will be less firm than Western custard. In fact, this dish is often classed as a soup. Sprinkle a little grated ginger on top before eating.

AWABI NO SAKA-MUSHI

(*Sake*-steamed Abalone)

INGREDIENTS (Serves 6)
6 fresh abalone, on the half-
  shell
2 tsp salt
3 tbsp *sake*

SAKE-STEAMING is one of the most common ways of making *mushimono*, and can be adapted to many different ingredients. If abalone is unavailable, you may steam clams — but remember to drastically reduce the steaming time (to about 3 minutes).

Preparation
Rinse the abalone shells thoroughly, scrubbing lightly with a medium-stiff brush to make certain all the sand is removed. Trim any

inedible growths from the edge of the shell or the abalone meat. Place the abalone, shell down, in a steamer.

Lightly salt the abalone and spoon amounts of *sake* over each one. Cover and bring the water to a high boil. Lower the heat slightly and steam for 20 to 25 minutes.

When the abalone are tender, remove them from their shells and discard the steaming water. Save the shells, as the meat is served on them. Make seven to eight slits in each abalone lengthwise (two-thirds in depth), and slice horizontally into ¼in thick pieces. Return the abalone slices to their shells arranging them in their original shape.

Mix together the *miso, mirin* water and the coloring agent over a low heat to make a green paste. When cool, brush the *miso* paste on the abalone.

Place an abalone in the shell on the bed of *harusame* and serve garnished with a lemon wedge and pickled ginger stems.

FOR GARNISH:
2oz white miso
2 tbsp mirin
3 tbsp water
few drops of coloring agent

FOR GARNISH:
4oz dried harusame soaked
in warm water for 5
minutes
lemon wedges
pickled fresh ginger stems

(Illustrated overleaf)

TAMAGO-DŌFU

(Egg 'Bean Curd')

THE JAPANESE are so fond of *tofu* that they like to reproduce it in as many ways as they can. This recipe represents a favorite way of eating *tōfu* (in a soy and bonito-flake sauce), only the *'tōfu'* in question is a delicious steamed-egg concoction.

Preparation

To prepare the egg *tofu*, beat the eggs thoroughly; stir in 2 cups (16fl.oz) of *dashi* and the salt. Pour the mixture into a small square baking dish (3½ cups/1½pt capacity) that has been lined with aluminum foil. Cover the top of the pan securely with another foil sheet. Steam for 4 minutes over a high heat in a steamer; lower the heat to medium and steam for 4 more minutes. Partially open the steamer lid and reduce the heat to low. Steam for 20 more minutes.

Release the egg *tofu* from the baking pan by carefully running a spatula or knife around the inside of the pan. Rest the bottom of the pan in ice-water. Cut the custard into six serving pieces. Cover the top of the pan with a plate, tip up, and release the custard from the mold. Chill the custard in ice-water or a refrigerator until ready to serve.

To make the sauce, combine the light soysauce, the *dashi*, the *mirin*, and *katsuo-bushi* flakes in a small saucepan. Bring to the boil, then remove from the heat and allow the sauce to cool to room temperature. This sauce may be used with real *tōfu* as well.

Top each *tōfu* square with a spoonful of sauce and sprinkle a little *sansho* pepper on top.

INGREDIENTS (Serves 6)
6 medium eggs
2 cups (16fl.oz) ichiban
dashi or niban dashi
1 tsp salt

FOR THE SAUCE:
1 tbsp light soysauce or 2 tsp
dark soysauce
6 tbsp ichiban dashi or
niban dashi
1 tbsp mirin (sweet cooking
sake)
1 tbsp dried, flaked katsuo-
bushi (dried bonito)

sansho pepper

(Illustration overleaf)

■ <u>AWABI NO SAKA MUSHI</u> (page 70)
　　Sake-steamed abalone
　　Garnish: <u>*sansho*</u> leaf

■ <u>TAMAGO-DŌFU</u> (page 71)
　　Egg 'bean curd'
　　Garnish: <u>*sansho*</u> leaf
　　(Illustration opposite top)

■ <u>CHAWAN MUSHI</u> (page 70)
　　Steamed custard
　　(Illustration opposite bottom)

SIMMERING (Nimono)

*T*here are a vast number of simmered dishes in Japanese cuisine. Many of them are extremely simple — merely ways of preparing a single fresh ingredient. A simmering liquid is allowed to flavor small pieces of vegetable for a few minutes. The heat is merely a means of fixing the flavor, for the dish is often allowed to return to room temperature.

UMANI

(Simmered Chicken)

INGREDIENTS (Serves 6)
1 whole chicken breast, boned and cut into bite-sized pieces
SAUCE:
1¹/₂ cups (12fl.oz) *ichiban dashi*
6 tbsp soysauce
3 tbsp *mirin*

2in section of *daikon*, peeled and cut into ¹/₂in × 1¹/₂in pieces
6 snow peas
1 medium size carrot, sliced and flower-cut (see page 36)
2 cakes of *koya-dōfu* (freeze-dried bean curd), soaked in warm water for 5 minutes
4oz crab meat
1 egg roll, cut into 6 (for instructions, see page 62)
STOCK FOR KOYA-DŌFU ROLLS:
1 cup (8fl.oz) *ichiban dashi*
¹/₂ tsp salt
1 tbsp soysauce

(Illustration overleaf)

INGREDIENTS ARE FIRST COOKED in separate pots and then simmered together briefly in seasoned stock just before serving.

Preparation
In a saucepan, mix together the chicken pieces, ¹/₂ cup (4fl.oz) *ichiban dashi*, 4 tbsp soysauce and 2 tbsp *mirin* and bring to the boil. Simmer for 10 to 15 minutes or until the chicken is cooked. Take off the heat and set aside.

Boil the *daikon* pieces in slightly salted water for 3 minutes and then add the snow peas. Cook for another 2 minutes. Remove the *daikon* and snow peas from the pan and set aside. In the same salted boiling water add the carrot 'flowers' and cook for 3 minutes.

Squeeze the excess water from the *koya-dōfu* cakes and slice both horizontally into two. Place a third of the crab meat on each of three of the slices (discard the fourth) and roll. Tie the edge of each *koya-dōfu* roll with a tooth pick. Mix the stock together in a saucepan and bring to the boil. Add the *koya-dōfu* rolls and simmer for 10 minutes. Drain and cut each into two.

Drain the cooked chicken and keep the sauce. In the sauce, add the remaining cup of *ichiban dashi* and season with the remaining tbsp of soysauce and of *mirin*. Bring to the boil and add all the ingredients: the chicken, *daikon*, snow peas, carrot, *koya-dōfu* and egg roll slices. Place an *otoshi-buta* on the ingredients and simmer for 3 minutes. Serve hot.

SABA NO MISO-NI

(Mackerel Simmered in *Miso*)

INGREDIENTS (Serves 4)
4 mackerel fillets, skin intact
salt
6in piece of *konbu* (kelp)
¹/₂ cup (4fl.oz) water
1in knob of fresh ginger
6 tbsp dark *miso*
5 tbsp *mirin*
2 tbsp *sake*

MISO IS A WONDERFUL SEASONING, and it works to good advantage in this recipe, accompanied by ginger.

Preparation
Rinse the fillets and pat them dry with paper towelling. Sprinkle the salt liberally over the fillets and let them stand for 10 to 15 minutes.

Blanch the fillets by adding them to vigorously boiling water. Keep boiling until the fillets are firm and white in color. Remove the fillets and put aside.

Put ½ cup (4fl.oz) water into a saucepan and add the *konbu*. Bring to the boil; remove the pan from the stove and discard the *konbu*. Peel ½ of the ginger and grate it. Pile up the gratings and gently squeeze them to obtain ginger juice. Add this juice to the water in which the *konbu* boiled. Slice the other half of the ginger into shreds and put them to soak in a little water.

Place the fillets in a skillet or a saucepan, large enough to allow them to lie in a single layer. Pour the *konbu* and ginger liquid over the fillets, drop an *otoshi-buta* on top, and simmer over a very low heat for 2 or 3 minutes.

In another, smaller saucepan, combine the *miso, mirin* and *sake* and cook over a moderate heat for about 1½ minutes, stirring constantly.

Add the *miso* sauce to the simmering mackerel liquid, stir, and cover again with the *otoshi-buta*. Simmer for about 4 more minutes, or until the sauce is shiny and not too plentiful.

Drain the ginger shreds and use them to top the dish. Serve warm or at room temperature.

(Illustration overleaf)

DAIKON NO ITAME-NI

(Simmered White Radish)

THE DAIKON (giant white radish) is one of the great 'workhorse' vegetables of the Japanese kitchen. Sliced, diced, curled as a bed for raw fish or grated as a garnish, the *daikon* is everywhere on Japanese menus, often somewhere on the margin of the main event, rather like a spear-carrier in an opera.

This dish gives the *daikon* a chance to shine, to prove what a subtly delicious vegetable it can be when it is allowed to take center stage.

INGREDIENTS (Serves 4)
8in section of *daikon*
½ tbsp vegetable oil
¾ cup (6fl.oz) ichiban dashi
3 tbsp mirin
1 tbsp sake
1½ tbsp soysauce

(Illustration overleaf)

Preparation

Peel the *daikon* and slice it either into rounds about ¾in thick, or into thin strips about 2in long. Heat the vegetable oil in a large saucepan. When a light haze can be seen above the oil, add the *daikon* slices and sauté them for about 2 minutes. Turn the slices over with a spatula or chopsticks and sauté the other side for another minute.

Add half the *dashi* and all the *mirin* and *sake*. Lower the heat and simmer for 5 minutes.

Add the remaining *dashi* and the soysauce; turn the slices over. Lower an *otoshi-buta* over the ingredients and simmer for about 5 minutes.

Turn the slices over once more, lower the *otoshi-buta* again and simmer until all the stock is absorbed. Check the *daikon*, however, in the final stages, and remove before they become overly soft.

■ SABA NO MISO-NI (page 74)
Mackerel simmered in *miso*
Garnish: *ginger shreds*

■ UMANI (page 74)
Simmered chicken and vegetables
(Illustration opposite top)

■ DAIKON NO ITAME-NI (page 75)
Simmered white radish
Garnish: *shreds of fresh chilli*
(Illustration opposite bottom)

TAKENOKO-NI (I)

(Simmered Bamboo Shoots)

INGREDIENTS (Serves 6)
1lb bamboo shoot
4-6 cups (32-48fl.oz) cold
   water
⅓ cup (⅓oz) rice-bran
   powder (nuka)
2 hot red peppers

THIS IS SIMPLY a way of bringing out the best in a smaller-sized (1lb) bamboo shoot. Bamboo shoots are symbols of springtime in Japan — they are sent forth in spring and the symbolism of growth and youth is obvious. Fresh bamboo shoots also possess a very subtle flavor, but by the time they reach market and your kitchen, their natural sweetness may have turned to a mild bitterness. This 'simmering' method freshens and restores them for eating as they are, or for inclusion in another dish.

Preparation

Select a bamboo shoot that still has some earth clinging to it and gives off a healthy, musky odor. Peel off a few of the outer leaves, and rinse — with plenty of water — to remove all the earth that may be stuck to the shoot. Cut off the top at a diagonal, make a shallow lengthwise cut along the side of the shoot, and cut straight across the base of the shoot, removing the bottom part. Rinse again. Now the shoot is prepared for simmering.

In a large saucepan, combine the water, rice-bran and the two peppers. Add the bamboo shoot and bring the water to the boil, then lower to a simmer. Lower an *otoshi-buta* to keep the bamboo shoot submerged during simmering. Simmer for 45 minutes to 1 hour.

Check to see if the shoot is cooked by pushing a toothpick into the core; it should go in easily. Remove from the water and peel off all the outer leaves. Trim the stubs of the leaves at the base of the shoot.

Slice into sections lengthwise, as you would slice a piece of fruit, and enjoy the shoot as it is; or leave the shoot whole and store it in a refrigerator, in enough cool water to cover it. Change the water every day; the bamboo shoot will stay good for about 10 days.

TAKENOKO-NI (II)

(Simmered Bamboo Shoots)

INGREDIENTS (Serves 6)
1 small bamboo shoot (about
   1lb)
1 large carrot
1 cup (8fl.oz) niban dashi
3 tbsp soysauce
½ tsp salt
3 tbsp mirin
12 snow peas

Fresh bamboo shoots are delicious simmered with vegetables in a soy-based sauce.

Preparation

Cook the bamboo shoot as in the recipe above. Cut into half lengthwise and slice each half into six to nine pieces, depending on the size of your bamboo shoot.

Scrape the carrot and boil for a few minutes until soft, but still crisp. Slice into six and 'flower-cut' all six pieces (see page 36).

Heat the *dashi* in a saucepan and add the soysauce, salt and *mirin*. Add the bamboo shoots and carrots. Place an *otoshi-buta* on the vegetables and simmer for 5 to 6 minutes or until the bamboo shoots become slightly brown.

Cook the snow peas in slightly salted water for 3 minutes and then drain.

In individual soup bowls place one sixth of the bamboo shoots, one flower-cut carrot piece and two snow peas. Pour a little juice from the saucepan into each bowl and serve either hot or cold.

(Illustration overleaf)

Ebi kimi-ni

(Simmered Shrimp)

WE RETURN TO SHRIMP in our survey of simple, basic Japanese food and cooking techniques. *Kimi-ni* means 'egg-yolk simmer', and it is egg yolk that supplies the glaze for the shrimp, while green beans are used as a garnish — the combination creates a lovely visual contrast of bright green and pink-tinted gold.

Preparation

Salt the shrimp lightly. Roll them in cornstarch, coating them well. Gently shake the shrimp to remove excess.

Bring 2 cups (16fl.oz) of water to a high boil. Add the shrimp and boil very briefly (about 10 seconds). Remove the shrimp from the water and rinse under cold running water. Set the shrimp aside.

Sprinkle salt over the beans. Bring 2 cups (16fl.oz) of water to the boil and add the beans. Boil for about 8 minutes, vigorously (without cover). The beans should become softer but still basically crisp. Drain and arrest further cooking by rinsing them under cold running water.

Prepare the stock for the green beans — combine the *dashi, mirin*, salt, *sake*, and soysauce in a saucepan. Bring the mixture to the boil and add the green beans. Allow the liquid to come to a second boil and, as soon as it does, remove the saucepan from the heat and set aside.

In another saucepan, prepare the sauce for the shrimp — combine the *sake, mirin, dashi*, and salt. Bring this mixture to the boil, add the shrimp, and return to the boil. Carefully pour the egg yolks over the shrimp. Cover the pan (do not use an *otoshi-buta*). Lower the heat and simmer for 2 minutes.

Remove from the heat and let rest for a few minutes. Drain the green beans and serve as a garnish alongside the shrimp.

INGREDIENTS (Serves 6)
18 medium shrimp, deveined
*   and shucked, with tails*
*   intact*
cornstarch
1lb green beans, trimmed
*   and cut on the diagonal*
*   into ¹/₂in pieces*
salt

STOCK FOR GREEN BEANS:
1 cup (8fl.oz) niban dashi
1 tbsp mirin
¹/₄ tsp salt
3 tsp sake
¹/₄ tsp soysauce

SAUCE FOR SHRIMP:
¹/₄ cup (2fl.oz) sake
1 tbsp mirin
6 tbsp niban dashi
¹/₂ tsp salt

4 egg yolks, beaten

■ TAKENOKO-NI II (page 78)
Simmered bamboo shoots with carrot and snow peas
Garnish: *sansho sprig*

DEEP-FRYING (Agemono)

*F*ried food in the Japanese style is a certain success with foreigners. Neither the restaurant favorite *tempura*, nor such less-familiar delicacies as chicken *tatsuta-age* seem strange to the Western taste-buds — they simply seem like logical improvements of familiar favorites.

The strong flavor of fried foods makes it possible to garnish them with spicy items like pickled ginger, the small Japanese green pepper (*ao-tōgarashi*) and the grated-radish-red pepper condiment called *momiji-oroshi*. Both *sanshō* pepper and 'seven spice pepper' (*shichi-mi tōgarashi*) are good sprinkled on the heartier deep-fried dishes. Fried foods are, like soup, meant to be eaten piping hot, right out of the oil.

KARA-AGE

(Deep-Fried Fish)

INGREDIENTS (Serves 4)
8 smelts or other small fish, cleaned
1/4 cup (2fl.oz) soysauce

DIPPING SAUCE:
3/4 cup (6fl.oz) ichiban dashi
1 tsp sake
1 1/2 tbsp soysauce
2 tbsp mirin

CONDIMENTS:
1 dried hot red pepper
1in piece of daikon (white radish) for grating
4 tbsp green onion, chopped finely

vegetable oil
1/2 cup (2oz) cornstarch
lemon wedges

(Illustration overleaf)

THE 'EMPTY FRYING' technique is perfect for fish. Here small, whole fish are treated in this simple and flavorful style. As with many Japanese deep-fried dishes, the actual frying produces a single sophisticated flavor that is then accented and highlighted by dipping sauces and garnishes.

Preparation

When the fish have been carefully cleaned and rinsed inside and out in plenty of water, cut a few decorative scores in the thicker part of the fish. Pour the 1/4 cup (2fl.oz) of soysauce over the fish and marinate for about 15 minutes.

Since the condiments in this recipe take a little time to prepare, it is a good idea to get them ready while the fish rest in the marinade.

Combine the *dashi, sake*, soysauce and *mirin* in a small saucepan and warm — do not boil. Keep warm while preparing the other condiments.

Poke several small holes around the middle of the peeled radish section. Cut open the red pepper, empty the small yellow seeds out, and discard them. Split the pepper into several strips and fit those strips into the holes in the *daikon*. Grate the *daikon* into a small bowl. The pepper flakes which appear in the radish mounds give this condiment its name: *momiji-oroshi* ('red-maple grate'). Chop finely some green onion and set aside.

Heat about 3in of oil in a heavy-botton saucepan or chip pan to around 350°F (mark 4). Dredge the marinated fish in cornstarch, coating lightly. Fry one fish at a time, for 5 to 6 minutes. Drain the fish on paper towels and keep warm until all are done.

Serve the fish on white absorbent paper with lemon wedges, and present the condiments in separate little dishes to each person. Everyone can then combine as much of each condiment as they want with the warm soy-based dipping sauce, and then dip the fish into the mixture.

AGEDASHI-DŌFU

(Deep-Fried *Tōfu*)

THIS DISH, like all really delicious *tōfu* dishes, has a simple, subtle taste, when eaten by itself; the dipping sauce and garnishes further complement the taste and add variety.

Preparation

First prepare the *tōfu* by pressing: drain the *tōfu* and wrap in a clean kitchen towel. Place two dinner plates on top of the *tōfu* and allow to stand for about 30 minutes before frying.

Put about 3in of vegetable oil into a chip pan or heavy-bottom saucepan and heat to 350°F (mark 4).

Cut the cakes of *tōfu* into halves and dredge lightly in flour. Deep-fry each half-cake separately, for 6 to 8 minutes or until golden. Keep skimming the oil surface to clean it. Place the fried *tōfu* on absorbent paper and drain briefly before serving.

Dipping sauce and garnish: Mix the *dashi, mirin* and soysauce together and warm in a small saucepan. If you wish to thicken this sauce, dissolve 1 tbsp cornstarch in 1 tbsp water and add to the sauce, stirring over the heat until the sauce has thickened.

Grate some *daikon* for each person and place it in a little individual dish; also provide a small mound of diced green onion for everybody. Other possible garnishes (each in its little dish or compartment) are grated ginger and dried bonito flakes (*katsuo-bushi*). Serve the *tōfu*; each person pours a little of the warm sauce (thick or thin) on top of the *tōfu* and tops it with scatterings of his/her choice of dry garnishes.

INGREDIENTS (Serves 4)
2 cakes of tōfu (use Chinese tōfu which is firmer in texture than Japanese tōfu)
oil for deep-frying
all-purpose flour

DIPPING SAUCE:
1¹⁄₃ cups (11fl.oz) ichiban dashi
2 tbsp mirin
2 tbsp soysauce
1 tbsp cornstarch

GARNISH:
1in section of daikon (white radish) for grating
4 tbsp green onion, chopped finely
1 tbsp cornstarch

(Illustration overleaf)

NANBAN-ZU

(Naban Vinegar)

THIS VINEGAR IS BEST when accompanying strongly-flavored food; it is also used as a marinade for whole-fish *tempura* or other deep-fried dishes.

Preparation

Mix the *mirin* with the vinegar in a saucepan over a medium heat, then add the soysauce and *dashi*. Bring just to the boil, then remove from the heat.

Seed the dried red chillis. Lightly broil the onions either in an oven or over charcoal. Cut into 2in lengths.

Add the chillis and onions to the vinegar mixture and simmer briefly over a moderate heat. Use this vinegar while it is hot.

INGREDIENTS
1¹⁄₂ tbsp mirin
¹⁄₂ cup (4fl.oz) rice wine vinegar
2 tbsp soysauce
²⁄₃ cup (6fl.oz) niban dashi
4 dried red chillis
4 green onions

■ <u>KARA-AGE</u> (page 82)
Deep-fried fish
Garnishes: <u>*shishito*</u> *pepper, lemon wedges,*
chopped green onion and <u>*momiji-oroshi*</u>

■ AGEDASHI-DŌFU (page 83)
Deep-fried *tōfu*
Garnishes: *chopped green onion and grated daikon*

TORINIKU TATSUTA-AGE

(Deep-Fried Chicken)

INGREDIENTS
6 tbsp sake
3 tbsp soysauce
2 tbsp green onion, finely
  chopped
small knob of fresh ginger
2lb chicken, boned, with skin
  attached
oil for deep-frying
flour

(Illustration overleaf)

鶏肉田揚げ

THIS RECIPE is a variation on the simple frying style *kara-age*, where no sort of breading or batter is used to coat the ingredients; a simple, light roll in flour is all that is required. *Tatsuta-age* chicken is, however, marinated first in a truly delicious soy-based sauce, before it is rolled in flour and deep-fried.

Preparation

Mix the *sake*, soysauce and green onion for the marinade. Peel and grate enough fresh ginger to make a small mound; gently press the gratings to produce ginger juice (you will need the equivalent of 1 tbsp. Add the ginger juice to the marinade.

Cut the chicken into bite-sized pieces and place in the marinade. Mix well, making sure that each piece is well-covered with the marinade. Marinate for 30 minutes.

For frying, use a heavy-bottomed saucepan and a generous amount of oil. Bring the temperature up to a moderate level (350°F/mark 4).

In a sieve, drain the excess marinade from the chicken pieces. Toss the pieces in flour, coating them lightly, and place on a plate to let the flour coating 'set' for a few minutes.

Put the chicken pieces into hot oil carefully, starting as close to the oil as you can (do not drop the pieces in from a height). Keep the pieces separate as you fry and keep the surface of the oil clean by regular skimming.

Transfer the chicken pieces to absorbent paper towelling as they finish frying. Keep them warm in your oven. Serve six or eight chicken morsels to each person on individual plates, or in small bamboo baskets, on a bit of absorbent paper.

FUKIYOSE

(Lightly Fried Shrimp and Vegetables)

INGREDIENTS (Serves 4)
12 shrimp, unshucked
24 ginkgo nuts, shucked
8 toothpicks
8 shishito peppers
2 eggplants
4oz harusame

(Illustration overleaf)

吹き寄せ

THE DISH, FUKIYOSE, is made up of a wide variety of little delicacies. This recipe is for a delicious mixture of lightly fried shrimp and vegetables.

Preparation

Wash and clean the shrimp, ginkgo nuts, *shishito* peppers and eggplants and pat dry with kitchen paper. Using eight toothpicks, place three ginkgo nuts on each one. Halve the eggplants and cut the round end off to make four bell-shaped pieces. On the skin-side of each eggplant half, make diagonal slits (¼in space in between each slit) so that the eggplant cooks quickly.

Heat the oil in a *tempura* pot or a wok to 325°F (mark 3), and deep-fry the *shishito* peppers for one minute. Drain the peppers well on kitchen paper. Increase the heat a little more, and then deep-fry the eggplant halves for a few minutes, or until they are cooked but still crispy. Drain on kitchen paper. Next, deep-fry the ginkgo nuts on their toothpicks for 2 minutes. Finally, deep-fry the shrimp for a minute or two. Drain both on kitchen paper.

On each of four plates, place three shrimp, two *shishito* peppers, two ginkgo nut sticks and one eggplant half. Eat with salt and soy-sauce.

KAKI-AGE

(Deep-Fried Pancakes)

THIS IS A FAIRLY COMPLEX DISH, unfamiliar to Western palates. Since *tempura* batter is used, it offers an interesting contrast with the more famous dish.

Preparation

Wash and trim the scallops (or any white fish) and cut into bite-sized pieces. Put these in a large bowl with the trefoil and onion pieces.

To make the *tempura* batter, combine the egg yolk, cold water and baking soda. Sift in 1²/₃ cups (6oz) flour and mix very slightly. The batter should look decidedly 'unmixed', with flour floating on top. Add to the other ingredients in the large bowl. Sift the additional ¼ cup (1oz) of flour over the bowl, and give the mixture a few strokes.

Using a large spoon, remove the pancake mixture a spoonful at a time and deep-fry for about 1 minute on each side in hot oil (see page 138 for detailed instructions on deep-frying). Drain each pancake by letting it rest briefly on absorbent paper towelling. Keep the pancakes warm while you prepare the eggplant.

Cut each eggplant into two. Cut off the round head of the eggplants to make a bell-shaped piece with the stem-side up. Make narrow slits in each eggplant. Lightly beat the egg yolks. Place the eggplant on a chopping board skin-side-up and press down with the palm so that each slit opens up slightly to make a fan shape. Keeping the shape, lift the eggplant 'fans' and dip ¼in from the bottom into the egg yolk. Deep-fry for 1 minute and drain.

To make a dip sauce, combine the *dashi*, soysauce, *mirin* and sugar and heat (do not boil) in a small saucepan, stirring to blend the mixture. Serve both an eggplant 'fan' and a *kaki-age* pancake to each person, garnished with grated ginger root on top of the grated *daikon*.

INGREDIENTS (Serves 6)
6 scallops (or ¹/₂lb white fish)
1 small bunch of trefoil, cut into 2in long pieces
2 naganegi (or 6 green onions), cut into half lengthwise and then into 1¹/₂in long sections

BATTER (makes 3 cups/ 24fl.oz):
1 egg yolk
2 cups (16fl.oz) water (ice-cold)
¹/₈ tsp baking soda
1²/₃ cups (6oz) flour
¹/₄ cup (1oz) flour
vegetable oil

3 small eggplants
3 egg yolks

DIPPING SAUCE:
1¹/₂ cups (12 fl.oz) niban dashi
3 tbsp soysauce
1 tbsp mirin
1¹/₂ tbsp sugar

GARNISH:
1 cup grated daikon
2-3 tsp grated fresh ginger

(Illustration overleaf)

■ <u>FUKIYOSE</u> (page 86)
　Lightly fried shrimp and vegetables, served on deep-fried *harusame*

■ <u>TORINIKU TATSUTA-AGE</u> (page 86)
　Deep-fried chicken
　Garnishes: *parsley and lemon slices*
　(Illustration opposite top)

■ <u>KAKI-AGE</u> (page 87)
　Deep-fried pancakes
　Garnishes: *grated ginger on grated <u>daikon</u>*
　(Illustration opposite bottom)

ONE-POT COOKING
(Nabemono)

One-pot cooking (*nabemono*) is a technique where everyone does their own cooking. An earthenware casserole (*donabe*) full of steaming stock, or a frying pan (for dishes such as *okaribayaki*, where the ingredients are pan-fried, not simmered) is placed in the centre of the table on a heating unit or gas ring. Platters of beautifully arranged meat, noodles and freshly cut vegetables are placed within easy reach. Each person is provided with spicy condiments and individual bowls of dipping sauces.

Nabemono are excellent dishes to do for parties. As all the ingredients can be prepared beforehand, the host/hostess is free to sit down with everyone else and join in the fun.

SHABU SHABU

(Hotpot)

THE NAME OF THIS DISH imitates the sound that is made as the ingredients are swished around in the steaming broth. Using chopsticks, everybody helps themselves from platters, decoratively arranged with fresh vegetables, *tōfu*, noodles and paper-thin slices of beef, and dips these ingredients into the communal pot (the high quality beef only needs to be dipped in the boiling stock for a few seconds). *Shabu shabu* is a great party dish, and is as popular among foreigners as it is with the Japanese.

Preparation

Neatly arrange the beef slices, one by one, on a large platter and garnish with a sprig of parsley in the center. On another large platter, carefully arrange the mushrooms, *tōfu*, Chinese cabbage, spinach and *harusame*. Skewer three ginkgo nuts on each of six toothpicks. Add these ginkgo nuts to the vegetable platter and garnish with lemon wedges and 'flower-cut' carrots. Place the *udon* in a *zaru* (bamboo dish) and garnish with a sprig of parsley.

Prepare the sauces and spicy condiments. To make the sesame paste sauce, blend all the ingredients together in an electric blender and divide into six small bowls. Give each person a small bowlful.

Pour 2 to 3 tbsp of soysauce into six small bowls and give one bowl to each person. Chop the green onion finely. Prepare the *momiji-oroshi* (see page 82). Place these condiments on the table so that everybody can mix them into the soysauce.

Place a piece of *konbu* in a large *donabe* casserole or *hōkō-nabe* (Mongolian hot-pot) and fill the pot three-quarters full of water. Place the pot on an electric heating unit or a portable gas ring on the table and bring the water to the boil. Take the *konbu* out and discard.

It is now time for everybody to help themselves to ingredients from the platters, to swish them around in the broth (in the case of the beef), or to drop them in and retrieve them later (in the case of the vegetables). Food just out of the pot should be dipped into either of the sauces and eaten immediately.

INGREDIENTS (Serves 6)
2lb beef (round steak), very thinly sliced
2 sprigs of parsley
1/4-1/2lb tightly curled mushrooms, cleaned
1 cake *tōfu*, cut into 6 or 12 pieces
3-4 Chinese cabbage leaves, washed and cut into 2 × 3in pieces
1/4-1/2lb spinach leaves, washed and trimmed
2-4oz *harusame*, soaked in warm water for 5 minutes
18 *ginkgo* nuts, shucked
6 lemon wedges
'flower-cut' carrots (see page 36)
1/2lb udon, cooked in boiling water for 8 minutes

SESAME PASTE SAUCE:
5oz white sesame seeds
1/2 cup (4fl.oz) soybean milk
3 tbsp soysauce
1 cup (8fl.oz) water
a drop of chilli oil

SOYSAUCE CONDIMENTS:
soysauce
3 tbsp *momiji-oroshi*
3 tbsp green onion

4in square konbu

(Illustration overleaf)

OKARIBAYAKI

(Duck One-Pot)

ALTHOUGH DUCK IS NOT a regular part of Japanese cuisine, dishes such as *okaribayaki* became part of Japanese eating via the tradition of open-air hunting cuisine. At Imperial and shōgunal shooting parties, kills were prepared on the spot so that hunters could enjoy the game immediately.

This dish falls into two categories of Japanese cooking. The ingredients are pan-fried (*yakimono* method) but the dish is also cooked by everybody at the table, making it a *nabemono*.

Preparation

Cut the boned breasts into strips about 3in long and ¼in wide, and set aside.

Remove the skin from the legs. Place the leg meat in a meat grinder or food processor and grind twice with the finest possible setting. Add the egg whites to the ground meat in a small bowl and beat together. When thoroughly mixed, form into balls about 1in in diameter.

Soak the *shiitake* mushrooms in cold water for about 30 minutes (if they are dried). Then sever and discard the stems and cut the mushroom caps in half.

Combine one egg yolk, the grated *daikon*, and the ½ tsp salt to make a dipping sauce. Give each person a small bowlful.

Seed, trim and slice the green pepper into strips. Peel the sweet potato and cut into 12 or so slices.

Arrange the duck meatballs, the meat strips, mushrooms, sweet potato and green pepper on a serving platter.

Place an electric skillet, or a heating unit plus a skillet, in the middle of a table, and oil the bottom of the skillet with a brush. Turn the heat to high. Test with a small piece of food and adjust the heat so that the food cooks promptly but not too quickly.

Put 8 tsp of soysauce in a large bowl, and position it near the serving table. Each person picks a piece of meat or vegetable, dips it into the soysauce, sautés it for 2 or 3 minutes, then drops it into the dipping sauce before eating.

INGREDIENTS (Serves 4)
5lb duckling, quartered and
*   with breasts and legs*
*   boned*
4 egg whites
4 shiitake mushrooms

DIPPING SAUCE:
1 egg yolk
1 cup (8oz) grated daikon
*   (white radish)*
½ tsp salt

1 green pepper
1 medium, sweet potato
vegetable oil
8 tsp soysauce

御狩場焼き

■ <u>SHABU SHABU</u> (page 90)
Beef and vegetables, cooked in broth
Dips: *soysauce and sesame sauce*
Garnishes: *chopped green onion and <u>momiji-oroshi</u>*

RICE (Gohanmono)

The Japanese have a special feeling for rice. Not only is this grain grown in almost every part of the country and eaten at almost every meal, for centuries it was also used as a standard of wealth — the *koku* (roughly equivalent to five bushels of rice) was the feudal stipend of Japan's *samurai* class. To this day, the rice-god, Inari, is a mainstay of the Shintō pantheon.

Lore and legend aside, we can say a few general things about Japanese rice. It is short-grained, polished and cooked in such a way that it coheres. Dry, separate grains, however appropriate they may be for Indian and English dishes, are not appreciated in Japan. Unhulled, or brown rice, is eaten in Japan, but it is associated with extreme poverty, or Buddhist asceticism. 'Real' rice for the Japanese, is the snowy-white variety — less nourishing certainly, but tastier and more elegant.

GOHAN

(Steamed rice)

INGREDIENTS

AMERICAN/EUROPEAN RICE:
1 cup (7oz) short-grain rice
1³/₄ cups (14fl.oz) water

JAPANESE RICE:
1 cup (7oz) rice
1 cup (8fl.oz) water

衛
飯

ANY SHORT-GRAIN RICE will make acceptable Japanese rice. If the rice you purchase was grown in the USA or Europe, it will require a little more cooking water (see ingredients below). The preparation will be otherwise identical.

Preparation

Wash the rice well about 1 hour before cooking — rinse several times, until the rice water has only the faintest milkness left. Drain in a strainer, and leave to stand for 1 hour.

When cooking time comes, place your rice in a saucepan that is neither so large that the rice is 'lost' in it, nor so small that the rice threatens to fill it — both extremes are dangerous to good taste and even cooking. Pour in the water and cover tightly. Turn the heat to medium and wait to hear the sound of low boiling. The cardinal rule of Japanese rice-making is to use your ears, not your eyes, to judge progress. Never lift the pot-lid to 'check' the rice. You will allow precious steam to escape.

When the rice boils, turn the heat to high. Soon the rice will be boiling merrily, and a whitish scum will begin to bubble up from under the lid. As soon as this begins to happen, reduce the heat to very low, and cook until you hear a faint, dry, popping sound, very different from the low, continuous bubbling of the simmering water.

Remove the saucepan from the heat at this point, and let the rice rest for 15 to 20 minutes, while retained heat continues to cook and retained steam acts to soften the rice. If you have not cheated on these rules — remember, no peeking — you should have perfect rice waiting for you when you lift the lid at last.

The Japanese manufacture automatic rice cookers that produce perfect rice almost without human intervention; by all means look for one of these in a Japanese goods or food shop. But remember, the point of Japanese cooking is not just to turn out food; it is to know and love the ingredients. To listen to the rice, to judge its progress, and finally to serve it as it should be served, will increase your feeling for the way the Japanese like to eat.

It is customary to transfer the rice to a rice tub and bring the tub, with its lid and paddle, to the table. There the host or hostess serves the guests in their individual rice bowls.

SEKIHAN

(Red Rice)

ONE OF THE MOST FAMILIAR and beloved of *gohanmono*, Red Rice is a popular holiday dish which is also served at weddings and other celebratory times. The sticky rice used here (*mochigome*) is the same grain that is used to make *mochi* (pounded-rice-cake), another holiday favorite. *Mochigome* is steamed, not boiled, and is undeniably sticky; the red beans impart a subtle flavor as well as the felicitous pink tint that gives the dish its name. Leave plenty of time to prepare it: the rice must soak in red-bean-tinted water for at least 4 hours.

INGREDIENTS (Serves 8)

½ cup (4oz) red beans (the small dried type used in many different national cuisines; there is no need to go to a Japanese food shop for these)

3 cups (21oz) mochigome (glutinous rice)

2 tbsp kuro-goma (black sesame seeds)

(Illustration overleaf)

Preparation

Rinse the beans thoroughly. Place them in a saucepan and cover them with 3 cups (24fl.oz) water; bring the water to the boil and simmer the beans uncovered for about 10 minutes, or until they have just begun to lose their hardness. Drain the beans, and reserve the cooking liquid, which will be pinkish in color.

Wash the *mochigome* thoroughly, several times; your final rinse-water should be completely clear, with no milky residue. Place the rice in another bowl and add half the pink-tinted cooking liquid from the red beans. Soak for about 4 hours at room temperature (if you refrigerate the rice, it should soak overnight). Do not discard the remaining cooking liquid.

Drain the rice and mix it with the beans. Spread the rice and beans evenly on a plate and then place it in a steamer. Steam the rice, covered, for about 15 minutes. Then remove the top and sprinkle the rice with a third of the remaining pink cooking liquid. Repeat the covered-steaming-and-sprinkling procedure two more times. The total steaming time will be about 45 minutes.

Remove from the heat and let the rice stand for a few minutes before serving. During this time lightly toast the black sesame seeds (without oil). Toast just long enough to release the sesame fragrance, taking care not to burn the seeds.

Toss the red rice a little with a spoon, and scatter the sesame seeds over the rice. This dish may be eaten warm, but it is more commonly enjoyed at room temperature.

■ <u>SEKIHAN</u> (page 95)
Red rice, served on top of bamboo leaves

■ <u>TORI-GOHAN</u> (page 98)
Chicken and rice
Garnish: *chopped <u>shiso</u> leaves*

TORI-GOHAN

(Chicken and Rice)

INGREDIENTS (Serves 4)
1¹/₂ cups (10oz) uncooked Japanese-type short-grain rice
1 whole chicken breast, boned and skinned
6 tbsp soysauce
1 tbsp sake
2 tbsp sugar
4 shiitake mushrooms (dried) — soak in water for about 30 minutes before use
4 cups (32fl.oz) niban dashi
4 tsp mirin
1 tsp salt
1 tsp soysauce
1 tbsp chopped parsley or shiso leaves

(Illustration previous page)

THIS HEARTY DISH of rice, chicken and mushrooms represents a straightforward Japanese rice dish. Any number of other good things may be substituted for the chicken and mushrooms — try peas and shrimp, or shredded clam meat.

Preparation

Wash the rice thoroughly and soak it in enough water to cover for about 3 hours.

Cut the chicken breast into strips 1in long and ¹/₈in wide.

Mix the 6 tbsp soysauce, the *sake* and sugar together and marinate the chicken strips in this mixture for half an hour.

Steam the *shiitake* mushrooms briefly (about 1 minute) and, while they are still hot, shred them as finely as possible.

Drain the soaking rice and add the *dashi, mirin*, salt and 1 tsp soysauce to it. Add the *shiitake*, and chicken strips. Bring to the boil, stirring a few times. Cover tightly and reduce the heat to medium; cook for 3 minutes. Bring the heat down to low and simmer for another 4 minutes. (Do not lift the lid to see how the rice is doing.)

Remove from the heat and let the rice sit, still covered, for a few minutes. Then garnish with chopped parsley or *shiso* leaves. You can serve this dish as a replacement for white rice at the end of a big meal, or as a light meal along with pickles and tea.

OYAKO DOMBURI

(Chicken-Egg-Omelet Rice)

INGREDIENTS (Serves 4)
8 cups (48oz) cooked rice
5 eggs
¹/₄lb chicken, boned and skinned
2 green onions (or 1 naganegi)
1 small bunch of trefoil
2¹/₂ cups (20fl.oz) ichiban dashi
9 tbsp soysauce
3 tbsp sugar

(Illustration overleaf)

THIS DISH, which is a real favorite everywhere in the country, has a whimsical and accurate Japanese name: *Oyako* means 'parent and child', and refers to the combination of the chicken and egg in an intimate 'family' relationship. *Domburi* dishes are big bowls of rice topped with something — omelet, fish or meat — the whole dish seasoned with soysauce.

Preparation

Boil the rice following the basic recipe on page 94; prepare the other ingredients as the rice rests, covered, and away from the heat. Mix the eggs together with a few strokes of a chopstick.

Cut the chicken into 1in and ¹/₄in wide pieces.

Wash the onions and cut on the diagonal into ¹/₂in lengths. Also, wash the trefoil and cut it into 1in lengths.

Combine the *dashi*, soysauce and sugar in a medium-sized saucepan. Bring to a moderate boil, and add the chicken; lower an *otoshi-buta* and simmer for about 5 minutes. Add the onion and trefoil and continue simmering for 1 minute longer.

Remove the *otoshi-buta* and pour the egg mixture into the pan, carefully distributing it around the chicken and vegetables. Do not stir; raise the heat to medium and allow the egg to cook until the edges bubble. Stir *once* to create a permanent 'swirl' effect. Do not overcook the egg, however; while it is still a bit moist and runny, remove the pan from the heat.

Divide the rice into four portions in four bowls (these should be deep bowls; the Japanese *domburi* bowl is, of course, the perfect choice).

Use a large spoon to 'carve out' a section of the omelet to fit on top of each bowl. The hot rice completes the cooking of the egg, making it tender and light; while the soysauce mixture in the egg filters downward and flavors the rice.

OCHAZUKE

(Tea and Rice)

THE JAPANESE THINK of *ochazuke* — the union of their traditional rice with their traditional tea — as about the most Japanese thing one can eat. This recipe spices up *ochazuke* just a little; the additional flavorings are, however, as traditional as the dish.

Preparation
Dry roast the sesame seeds until they are lightly golden — be careful not to burn them.

Distribute the rice equally between four bowls. You may top each bowl with a sprinkle of sesame seeds or serve the seeds separately.

Pass the sheet of *nori* back and forth a few times over a direct moderate heat to freshen its taste. Fold or cut into about 20 small pieces and lay five on each mound of rice. Distribute the pieces of trefoil equally between the four bowls.

Give each person a small dish containing a little mound of *wasabe* and, if you choose, some of the lightly roasted sesame seeds, which they can add to their rice according to taste.

Pour ½ cup (4fl.oz) of hot green tea over each bowl and then serve.

To vary this recipe, you may add strips of leftover meats or fish before adding the tea. A particularly nice version is *sake no ochazuke* (salmon and rice tea).

INGREDIENTS (Serves 4)
1 tbsp white sesame seeds
  (shiro-goma)
3 cups (18oz) short-grain
  rice, cooked Japanese style
  (see page 94)
1 sheet dried nori (laver)
small bunch trefoil, chopped
  into 1in pieces
2 level tsp powdered wasabe,
  mixed with a little water
  into a smooth paste
2 cups (16fl.oz) hot green tea

(Illustration overleaf)

■ <u>OYAKO DOMBURI</u> (page 98)
Chicken and egg on rice
Garnish: *shredded <u>nori</u>*

■ <u>OCHAZUKE</u> (page 99)
Tea and rice
Garnishes: *<u>wasabi</u> horseradish and white sesame seeds*
(Illustration opposite top)

■ <u>SAKE NO OCHAZUKE</u> (page 99)
Salmon and rice tea
Garnishes: *<u>wasabi</u> horseradish and white sesame seeds*
(Illustration opposite bottom)

SALADS (Aemono and Sunomono)

hese delicate combinations of ingredients with cold sauces are either served in minute portions just before the start of a meal, as a *zensai* ('beginning dish'), or near the end of a meal.

There are two basic types of 'salads': *sunomono* (vinegared things) and *aemono* (mixed things). Although it is not a hard and fast rule, the dressings for *sunomono* are generally thin and vinegar-based, while the *aemono* dressings are thicker and have either toasted and ground sesame seeds, *tōfu* or *miso* as their base.

In these dishes, fish, shellfish and practically any vegetable, either raw or cooked, are combined together and tossed with a dressing to produce complex, imaginative, and often exotic, flavors. It is better if you can serve small amounts of several of these 'salads' rather than a full Western-type portion of any of any one of them.

KYŪRI TO WAKAME NO SUNOMONO

(Cucumber and Seaweed Salad)

INGREDIENTS (Serves 4)
1oz bunch dried wakame
seaweed
4 tbsp rice-wine vinegar
3 tbsp soysauce
2 tsp sugar
1 cucumber
½ tsp salt

(Illustration overleaf)

胡
瓜
と
わ
か
め
の
酢
の
物

SPRING IS THE TIME when the *wakame*, or 'young seaweed' can be found in Japanese waters. This recipe is another 'classic' sort of *sunomono*; the saucing is even simpler than in the *kanisu* recipe (opposite) giving the *wakame* the chance to take center stage.

Preparation

Fill a large bowl with warm water and soak the *wakame* seaweed for about half an hour. The seaweed will expand rather dramatically in volume. After soaking, remove the seaweed from the bowl, rinse under cold running water, and pat dry using kitchen towelling. Remove the stems and chop coarsely; do not make the pieces too small.

Combine the vinegar, soysauce and sugar in a small saucepan. Heat the mixture until the sugar is entirely dissolved. Then immediately remove from the heat and chill.

Peel the cucumber; you can do it decoratively by leaving very thin unpeeled strips along its length at regular intervals. Slice the cucumber in half lengthwise and scoop out the seeds. Slice each half lengthwise, very thinly. Dissolve the salt in ½ cup (4fl.oz) of cold water, and soak the cucumber slices for about 20 minutes. Drain, and gently press out excess moisture from the cucumber with kitchen towelling.

Combine the cucumber slices and chopped seaweed. Pour the vinegar dressing over the whole salad and toss gently, taking care not to damage the cucumber slices.

Serve either chilled or at room temperature; somewhere in-between is probably ideal.

KANISU (I)

(Vinegared Crab)

THIS IS A SIMPLE and quite typical *sunomono*; typical in that it combines cucumber and seafood and uses the *sambai-zu* sauce — a mixture of soy and vinegar, with *dashi*. As we progress from dish to dish in this survey of basic 'national' techniques and tastes, note the recurrence of such mainstays as *dashi* and soy; unlike French cuisine, for example, where sauces are rich and complex, Japanese cooks rely upon familiar and simple sauces to highlight the variety of fresh ingredients on hand.

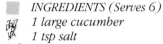

INGREDIENTS (Serves 6)
1 large cucumber
1 tsp salt
12oz crab meat
3 tbsp ginger root, grated

SAMBAI-ZU SAUCE:
2¹/₂ tbsp rice wine vinegar
2¹/₂ tbsp niban dashi
4 tbsp mirin
2 tsp soysauce
¹/₈ tsp salt

Preparation
Peel the cucumber and cut it in half lengthwise. Scoop out the seeds with a small spoon. Slice the cucumber halves crosswise as thinly as you can; it is important for the appearance of the finished dish to make these slices almost paper-thin.

Dissolve 1 tsp of salt in ¹/₂ cup (4fl.oz.) of cold water and add the cucumber slices. Soak them for about 20 minutes, then drain and gently work out the excess moisture with a kitchen towel.

Shred the crab meat into the thinnest possible filaments, picking out any bone or cartilage in the process.

Distribute the crab and cucumber to individual bowls and arrange it artistically. Wrap the grated ginger in a section of cheesecloth and squeeze a few drops of ginger juice over the ingredients.
To make the sauce: Combine all the ingredients in a small saucepan. Bring to the boil, stirring constantly. As soon as the sauce has begun to boil, remove it from the heat and set it aside to cool.

Serve this sauce in a small separate bowl, allowing people to use it as a dipping sauce.

KANISU (II)

(Vinegared Crab)

Preparation
Having cooked the crab meat, remove it carefully from the crab claws, trying to keep the claws intact. Shred the crabmeat finely.

Combine the *mirin*, vinegar, soysauce and *dashi*. Bring to the boil and immediately remove from the heat. Allow to cool to room temperature. Season with the ginger juice.

Place a mound of crab meat on each of four small plates. Spoon 2 tbsp of the ginger and vinegar sauce on each portion. Decorate with the claws and, if you wish, garnish with lemon wedges. Serve chilled.

INGREDIENTS (Serves 4)
6oz steamed or boiled crab
    meat in the shell
³/₄ tbsp mirin
¹/₄ cup (2fl.oz) rice vinegar
1 tbsp soysauce
¹/₃ cup ichiban dashi
2 tsp (3fl.oz) fresh ginger
    juice

(Illustration overleaf)

■ <u>KANISU II</u> (page 103)
Vinegared crab
Garnishes: *bamboo leaves, lemon wedges and lime slices*

■ KYURI TO WAKAME NO SUNOMONO (page 102)
Cucumber and seaweed salad

NASU NO AN-KAKE

(Eggplant Salad)

INGREDIENTS (Serves 4)
¹/₂ lb ground meat
pinch of salt and pepper
vegetable oil
3 shiitake mushrooms, soaked
*   in warm water for 30*
*   minutes, and finely*
*   chopped*
3 tbsp sake
5 tbsp dark miso
3 tbsp sugar
4 small eggplants
4 snow peas, boiled for 2-3
*   minutes, drained and*
*   chopped finely*

(Illustration overleaf)

茄
の
あ
ん
か
け

IT MAY BE STRETCHING the category of salads a bit to include an *an-kake* dish; nevertheless, this, like *sunomono* and *aemono*, is a simple dish accompanied by a sauce, and served at room temperature. Small Japanese eggplants are used, as well as *miso* (bean paste), which lends its hearty flavor to the interesting and tasty sauce.

Preparation

Season the ground meat with salt and pepper. Heat a small amount of oil in a skillet and stir-fry the ground meat. Add the *shiitake* and stir-fry further until the meat and *shiitake* are cooked.

In a saucepan, combine the *sake*, *miso* and sugar over a low heat. Add the sautéed ground meat and *shiitake* mixture and set aside, keeping warm.

Cut each eggplant in half lengthwise. Make a few slits on the skin. Heat the vegetable oil to a moderate heat (about 325°F/mark 3). Deep-fry each eggplant half individually, starting with the skin-side down. Fry for 1 or 2 minutes on the skin side, then turn and fry the other side for 3 to 4 minutes. The eggplant should turn golden brown and the flesh should separate a little from the skin. Test for tenderness with a toothpick; the toothpick should slide in easily. Drain the eggplant thoroughly on absorbent towelling.

Place two halves of eggplant on an individual plate and top with some of the ground meat and *miso* sauce. Serve garnished with the finely chopped snow peas.

GOMA JŌYU-AE

(Sesame-Soybean Salad)

INGREDIENTS (Serves 6)
1 lb green beans
1 cup (8fl.oz) niban dashi
2 tsp sake
1 tbsp sugar
¹/₄ tsp soysauce

DRESSING:
¹/₂ cup (4oz) white sesame
*   seeds*
2 tsp sugar
3 tbsp sake
2 tbsp soysauce

胡
麻
醤
油
和
え

HERE IS A VARIATION on the sesame theme, this time with green beans. *Sake* helps give this dish its intriguing taste; and the sesame adds a pleasantly nutty quality.

Preparation

Trim the green beans and cut them on the diagonal at ¹/₂in intervals. Bring 2 cups (16fl.oz) of lightly salted water to the boil and drop in the beans. Boil uncovered for about 9 minutes, or until the beans are tender but not soft, and still resist your bite. Drain and run cold water over the beans to arrest cooking by retained heat.

In a saucepan, combine the *dashi*, 2 tsp *sake*, 1 tbsp sugar, and ¹/₄ tsp soysauce. Bring to the boil after mixing well. Add the beans and allow to return to the boil. As soon as it has done so, remove the pan from the heat and allow to return to room temperature.

Dressing: It is first necessary to burn off the alcohol in the 3 tbsp of *sake*. Heat the *sake* in a small saucepan until it is fragrant. Remove the saucepan from the heat and ignite the fumes of the wine with a match. Allow the flame to burn out, while occasionally shaking the saucepan gently. Allow the *sake* to cool.

Toast the sesame seeds without oil in a small skillet, until they are golden brown. Take care that they do not roast and turn too dark. Transfer the sesame seeds to a Japanese grinding-bowl (*suribachi*) and grind vigorously, turning the seeds into a paste.

Add the *sake*, 2 tbsp of soysauce, and 2 tsp of sugar to the sesame paste in the *suribachi*, and, using the pestle, mix well.

Transfer the dressing to another bowl, drain the green beans, add them to the dressing, and toss thoroughly, making sure all the beans are coated. Serve in small bowls, at room temperature.

(Illustration overleaf)

TORIWASA

(Chicken-*Wasabi* Salad)

WASABI PASTE is the pungent mustard made from the ground root of the *wasabi*, a plant native to Japan. The nickname for *wasabi* in *sushi* shops (where it is an important garnish) is *namida*, 'tears', and eating a little too much of this bright-green condiment will bring more tears to your eyes than chopping an onion. This does not prevent *wasabi* from being one of the most intriguingly delicious of all Japanese spices.

INGREDIENTS (Serves 6)
1 tbsp grated *wasabi* root, or canned *wasabi* powder
1 dried *shiitake* mushroom, soaked in water for about 30 minutes
1 whole chicken breast, boned, skinned and sliced into very fine shreds
salt
6 tbsp *sake*
1 bunch parsley
2¹/₂ tbsp soysauce

(Illustration overleaf)

Preparation

Add enough water to the *wasabi* to make a thick paste, and let it rest for 15 minutes. Drain and dry the mushroom, then slice it into thin strips. In a small saucepan, combine the chicken, mushroom strips, ¹/₈ tsp of salt, and the *sake*. Bring to the boil over a moderate heat and set to one side, cool to room temperature.

In another pan, boil ¹/₂ tsp of salt and 1¹/₂ cups (12fl.oz) of water, and add the parsley. Boil the parsley for 1 minute, then drain. To enrich the color and arrest cooking, rinse the parsley under cold running water. Gently squeeze out the moisture from the parsley, pat dry with kitchen towelling and chop coarsely. Set aside.

Combine the chicken and mushrooms in their liquid, and the chopped parsley with 2¹/₂ tbsp of soysauce. Stir and toss together until thoroughly mixed.

Divide the salad into six small bowls, and top each one with a cone of *wasabi* paste. Serve at room temperature.

■ <u>NASU NO AN-KAKE</u> (page 106)
Eggplant salad
Garnish: *finely chopped snow peas*

108

■ TORIWASA
(page 107)
Chicken salad
Garnish: *wasabi
horseradish paste*

■ GOMA JŌYU-AE
(page 106)
French-style green
bean salad in a soy
and sesame sauce

HŌRENSO NO GOMA-AE

(Spinach Salad with Sesame Dressing)

INGREDIENTS (Serves 4)
1 lb (16oz) fresh spinach
4 tbsp white sesame seeds
1 tsp sugar
2 tsp soysauce
3 tbsp dashi

(Illustration overleaf)

YOUNG, VERY FRESH Western spinach will make a good substitute in this dish. Japanese spinach is rather more delicate in both taste and texture, however, and if you can find it at a Japanese food shop, so much the better.

Preparation

Bring to the boil enough salted water to cover the spinach; add the spinach and boil briefly, until its color deepens and the leaves begin to wilt. Drain and chop the spinach into strips about 1½in long. Set aside.

Toast the sesame seeds lightly, without oil, in a small pan. Toast until the seeds are golden and fragrant. Place the seeds in a Japanese grinding bowl (*suribachi*) and grind them until they are coarsely crushed. Add the sugar and stir, using the pestle. Add the soysauce and the *dashi*. Mix all the ingredients well, stirring very rapidly.

Add the spinach and mix well with the dressing, using light pressure. Crush the spinach leaves only slightly, making sure the dressing soaks into them.

This is a very common salad in Japan, where it is served in little, deep bowls. The flavor emerges best if the salad is served at room temperature.

An alternative way of serving this salad is to divide the spinach into three portions, after having mixed it with the dressing. Then using a *sudare* mat, roll each portion into a cylinder shape and top with some more white sesame seeds.

KŌHAKU NAMASU

(Red and White Vinegared Salad)

INGREDIENTS (Serves 12)
8in length of daikon (white
*   radish)*
2 medium carrots
1 tsp salt
½ cup (4fl.oz) rice wine
*   vinegar*
2½ tbsp mirin
½ cup (4fl.oz) dashi
1½in square of konbu (kelp)

(Illustration overleaf)

THIS COLORFUL SALAD of carrot (which is considered 'red' for purposes of this dish) and *daikon* offers a visually pleasant variation on the standard *sunomo*.

Preparation

Scrape the *daikon* and carrot. Cut the vegetables into rectangular blocks, then slice them into paper-thin small rectangles (see directions for the *tanzaku-giri* cut, page 32).

Put all the vegetable pieces into one large mixing bowl and sprinkle with 1 tsp of salt. Allow to stand for 10 minutes, then knead the vegetables gently with your fingers. The *daikon* strips should become translucent. Using kitchen towelling, gently press out as much moisture as you can from the vegetables. Place the vegetables in a clean bowl.

Combine the rice wine vinegar, the *mirin* and *dashi* in a small saucepan. Bring the mixture to the boil, then remove from the heat and let it cool down. (This will produce 1 full cup (8fl.oz) of *amazu*, or 'sweet vinegar'.)

Add ¼ cup (2fl.oz) of the vinegar mixture to the vegetables. Mix the vinegar and vegetables thoroughly, then press out the vinegar with your hands or a towel and discard the vinegar.

Add ½ cup (4fl.oz) additional vinegar mixture to the vegetables and mix. Cover the vegetables with the *konbu* sheet, then cover the bowl itself and refrigerate. For best taste, the salad should rest overnight; in any case, leave it in the refrigerator as long as feasible in order to allow the *konbu* flavor to subtly permeate the vegetables.

SHIRAZU-AE

(White Salad)

PUREED TOFU (bean curd) is an important ingredient in this thick dressing. Indeed, *tōfu* is perhaps the most adaptable of all the many multi-purpose Japanese 'basic foods' — it appears as a main dish, a side dish and a snack; it is used in soups and sauces.

Preparation

Soak the mushrooms, in enough warm water to cover, for about 30 minutes to 1 hour. Remove the mushrooms (which will have swollen in size and become soft), dry, and cut them into thin julienne strips (*sen-giri* technique — see page 32).

Cut the carrot into similar small strips, boil for a few minutes and drain. Blanch the French-style green beans in a small amount of boiling water for about 3 minutes, then drain and allow the vegetables to return to room temperature.

In a small pan, combine the *dashi*, sugar and soysauce and heat until the sugar is dissolved. Add the carrot, mushrooms and French-style green beans and simmer (using an *otoshi-buta*) for about 15 minutes. Drain the vegetables and allow them to cool.

Put the *tōfu* in a saucepan with enough water to cover; bring to the boil and boil for no longer than 3 minutes. Line a strainer or colander with cheesecloth and drain the *tōfu*. Pick up the *tōfu* cake in the cheesecloth and squeeze the moisture out thoroughly. Mash the *tōfu* in a large bowl, then add the other dressing ingredients: the sugar, *sake*, salt, a few drops of soysauce (be very sparing), the *mirin* and the vinegar. Mix very thoroughly.

Add the white dressing to the vegetables and toss thoroughly. Serve this salad with one of the simpler cucumber *sunomono*.

INGREDIENTS *(Serves 4)*
6 dried shiitake mushrooms
1 medium size carrot
4 oz French-style green beans
⅓ cup (3fl.oz) niban dashi
2 tbsp sugar
2 tbsp soysauce

DRESSING:
½ cake tōfu
1¼ tbsp sugar
½ tsp sake
1 tsp salt
few drops soysauce
½ tbsp mirin
½ tbsp rice-wine vinegar

(Illustration overleaf)

■ **HŌRENSŌ NO GOMA-AE** (page 110)
Spinach salad with sesame dressing

■ **KŌHAKU NAMASU** (page 106)
Red and white vinegared salad
Garnish: *citrus peel*
(Illustration opposite top)

■ **SHIRAZU-AE** (page 111)
Vegetables with *tōfu* dressing
(Illustration opposite bottom)

REGIONAL

DISHES

Regional introduction
Kyūshū and the Inland Sea
The Kansai
Tokyo and the Kantō
The North

地方料理

REGIONAL INTRODUCTION

*T*here are many ways to arrange Japanese food beautifully upon a plate, but one technique has always seemed to me a special symbol of Japan itself. In this technique, the cook places large, round foods further away from the person, in the 'background' of the plate, and smaller, more finely cut things in front. For anyone who has looked at the Japanese landscape, it makes immediate sense. It is a little diorama, repeating the most typical landscape view in Japan — a foreground of paddies, rice sheaves, buildings, water, bridges, and the eternal background of the low, rolling green hills.

The very fact that such a diorama can represent Japan tells us much about the country. Whereas China, with its many languages and its vast and varied stretches of land, is very much a world unto itself, Japan is very much a nation, conscious of its compactness, and assertive of its traditions, well aware that it is on the periphery of a continental colossus with an overwhelming culture.

Differences of geography, climate, and ways of life are far less pronounced in the island country than in China, and yet geography has chanced to create perhaps more regional diversity than is common in countries of Japan's size (it measures 145,824 square miles/— slightly larger than Norway). For Japan is also 80 percent mountainous, and mountainous countries tend to preserve localisms of all sorts.

One of the strongest local traditions throughout Japan is cooking. Local products not only thrive in their native localities, but have also spread throughout the nation. Train travelers can enjoy *ekiben* (train-station lunches) that are selected specialties of the region through which they are traveling — and there are regional restaurants in all the great cities. Most important of all, the hundreds of national guide-book series turned out by Japan's prodigious publishing industry advise domestic tourists which product tastes best where, and visitors never fail to pick up a package of the special local pickle or the dried fish snack *du pays* to bring back home as a gift for friends and co-workers.

The Tokugawa Shōgunate
As I noted in the Introduction, Japanese regional eating resembles other local Japanese traditions in being a matter of a few altered elements, not separate worlds of experience. To understand why, we should turn to Japanese history; this is a tale of continuous national unification. A succession of strong rulers succeeded in imposing more and more uniformity upon the mountains and river valleys and rice-growing plains of this island country. Their crowning achievement was the 300 years (1600-1868) of centralized feudalism under the Tokugawa *shōguns*, or generals.

The Tokugawa created a national economy, improved transportation in important ways, vastly increased the national

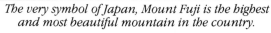

*The very symbol of Japan, Mount Fuji is the highest
and most beautiful mountain in the country.*

Sea of Japan

THE KANSAI

Wakasa · Kyoto · Kosuga · Shiga

Iwakuni · OSAKA · NA

HIROSHIMA

KITA-KYŪSHŪ · Shimonoseki

SAGA · FUKUOKA · BEPPU

Yawata · Tosa

NAGASAKI

KYŪSHŪ · Satsuma

KYŪSHŪ AND THE INLAND SEA

consciousness of the Japanese, and, in general, laid many of the foundations for the creation of a modern nation-state called Japan in the late nineteenth century. In 1868 a reform movement, centered around a new theory of the sovereignty of the Emperor (who had taken a back-seat to feudal generalissimos for centuries), overthrew the Tokugawa and set Japan upon a course of modernization and competition with Europe and America.

We owe much of the preservation of Japanese localism and regionalism to the Tokugawa era of extreme conservatism in social and political matters. Had Japan continued fighting the sort of devastating feudal wars that preceded the Tokugawa, there might

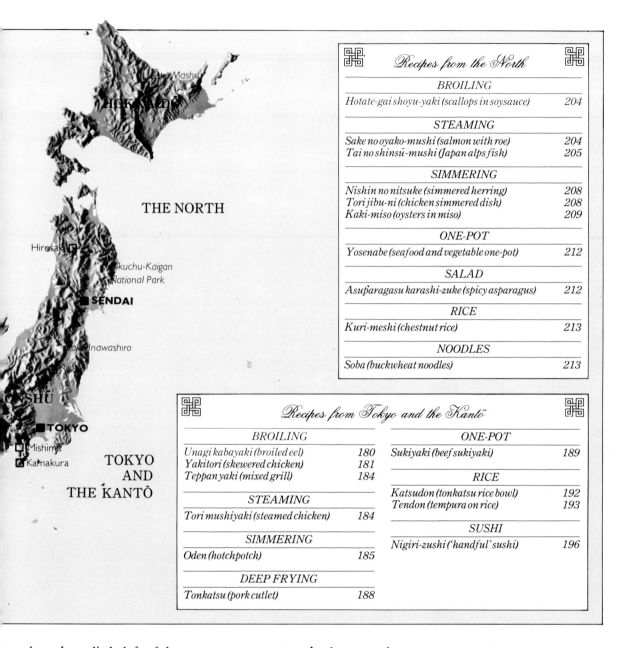

have been little left of the country to preserve. At the same time, important traditions in art, culture, and even cuisine grew up in spite of Tokugawa authority. The great cities of Ōsaka and Edo (and, to a lesser extent, Kyōto), challenged the rather numbing authority of the Tokugawa by producing some of the most vibrant of all pre-modern city cultures. Popular theatre, music, art and poetry exploded from the licensed brothel quarters of the cities, giving birth to such familiar and by now 'classic' Japanese arts as the *kabuki* and the woodblock print. Great restaurants were an important part of this unofficial urban renaissance, and many of the finest establishments in Japan today proudly trace their ancestry

With the land mass of Japan split into four main islands and nearly 4,000 islets, and a coastline of 18,450 miles, water is central to the Japanese way of life — literally so in the case of the Inland Sea (top), a strip of sea bordered by three of the main islands. On the fourth island, Hokkaido, Lake Mashu (above) is said to be the clearest lake in the world. The fish market (right) shows some of the many types of fish supplied by the lakes, the rivers and the seas.

back to the Tokugawa period, when good taste and stylish eating were as much a part of the life of the city dandy as elegant kimono linings and expensive tobacco-pipes.

Modern Japan

When Japan turned toward the modern world after 1868, the great Japanese cities had a head start toward becoming the conurbations they are today. Not only foreign ideas, but foreign and foreign-derived products of every description flooded big Japanese cities, and modern 'traditions', such as the beer hall, the *sukiyaki* store and the National Diet (Parliament), grew up, even while the countryside lovingly preserved its old institutions. Romantic nationalism periodically helped preserve and publicize 'old Japan', and the

Cultivable land is at a premium, with rice taking the lion's share. Planting (left) takes place in spring, and the annual crop is far in excess of domestic needs. The lowlands near Mishima, with Mount Fuji in the background (above) are also used for other crops, including tea, wheat, barley and vegetables.

complex mixture of the new and old that is still to be seen in the country became the norm of Japanese culture.

Hence, our tour of Japanese regional specialties necessarily involves us in Japanese history. In Kyūshū, we can taste dishes so simple and primordial that they are probably little changed from the medieval era — and we can eat *tempura*, which came to the country with missionary Jesuits and Portuguese traders. In Tokyo we will sample a kind of *sushi* the origin of which goes back beyond the Tokugawa era — and *sukiyaki*, the 'European' beef dish that was very popular with the smart student set in the 1880s.

For the purpose of our tour, four regions sum up the major divisions in Japanese eating and cooking: Kyūshū and the Inland Sea, the Kansai, the Kantō and the North.

KYŪSHŪ AND THE INLAND SEA

Kyūshū, southernmost of Japan's main islands, is something of a paradox. Historically the oldest of the islands, it is today a center of high technology. Infertile land has kept much of the island agriculturally backward and culturally provincial, yet Nagasaki was for centuries Japan's most cosmopolitan city, and Kyūshū feudatories took the lead in pulling Japan into the modern world after 1860. Abandoned coal mines, legacies of the nation's early modernization, pit the landscape of central Kyūshū, while the northern end of the island hums with heavy industry.

PERHAPS THE ONE QUALITY of Kyūshū culture that can account for all its inconsistencies is simply a proud sense of independence. Kyūshū people are aware of the important contributions they have made to the development of Japan, old and new, while at the same time they treasure the traditions and habits that distinguish them from their countrymen to the north and east. North Kyūshū, dominated today by the cities of Fukuoka and Kita-Kyūshū, was the birthplace of Japanese civilization, the place where horse-riding aristocrats from the Asian mainland first came ashore to begin the eastward conquest of the Japanese land.

Indeed, Kyūshū's position as the gateway to the continent and to the southern seas has often pulled it away from the centers of national authority and culture. In the eighth century, the northern part of the island saw the growth of a truly cosmopolitan, heavily Chinese-influenced school of poets. Contacts with journeying Europeans in the sixteenth century made Nagasaki one of the most important Catholic cities of Asia, and a workshop for new technology and ideas. Japan's unifiers, increasingly inward-looking, could not help but see Kyūshū as a problem region, where proud lords, used to independence in religion and foreign policy, posed a threat to the changeless order that the unifiers intended.

The Tokugawa regime (1603-1868) enforced severe strictures against the entry of foreign goods and foreign ideas. And yet, when the intellectual ropes were loosened slightly in 1720, and the importation of foreign books was allowed, Nagasaki once again became the center for foreign ideas and influences. As the Tokugawa order crumbled, the lords of Kyūshū were prominent first in the movement to restore Imperial rule, and then in the whirlwind of enthusiasm for European technology that finally transformed Japan intellectually as well as politically.

When it comes to eating, Kyūshū is both sturdily Japanese and irrepressibly outward-looking. Seafood, often the finest item on a Japanese menu, is eaten in abundance here thanks to the quantity of fish in the waters off North Kyūshū. The king of the Japanese fishes, *tai* (sea bream) thrives in these waters, as does the turbot (*karei*) and that most dangerous of all delicacies, blowfish (*fugu*), which is delicious cooked just right, and deadly poisonous when underdone.

The Chinese traditions of Nagasaki have elevated a rather un-Japanese meat, pork, into prominence in Kyūshū cooking and led

The majestic torii (entrance gate) to the Shinto shrine of Itsukushima is the largest in Japan and is set in the waters of Hiroshima Bay. Until the Mej ji restoration in 1867, births and deaths were not allowed to spoil the purity of the sacred island. The small shiitake mushrooms (inset) are gathered in spring and autumn. Available dried, they can be reconstituted by a short soaking.

A pool of blood-red mud, one of the hot springs (onsen) near the famous sea-side resort of Beppu. There are more than 3,000 springs, producing millions of gallons of near-boiling water every day, which serve the town and the nearby health spas. Onsen are part of the continuous volcanic activity in Japan.

to the creation of *shippoku* cuisine, an ingenious blend of Chinese and Japanese food. The Spanish and Portuguese, who lived in Nagasaki in the 1500s, also introduced a style of cooking — a type of deep-frying — that has further enriched Kyūshū's culinary range. Meanwhile, traditional specialties are not neglected — both *shiitake* mushrooms and *daikon* (white radish) are found at their best on Kyūshū.

The Inland Sea

The factories of Kita-Kyūshū mark the beginning of a heavy industrial corridor that stretches all the way to Tōkyō in the east. For much of its length, this great belt of industry parallels one of the Earth's loveliest regions, the 350-mile-long *Seto Naikai*, the 'sea within the channels', or Inland Sea. Bordered on the west by Kyūshū, on the north by Honshū (where the industry is) and on the south by Japan's smallest and most rural island, Shikoku, the Inland Sea is a magnificent saltwater setting for about 1,000 islands of all sizes and shapes. Here, increasingly threatened by industrial pollution, live an enormous variety of fish and shellfish. Historically, the waterway was used by the conquering Kyūshū chieftains and their followers to make their way eastward. When they reached land at the eastern end of the *Seto Naikai*, they entered what was to become the heartland of a new culture — the Kansai Plain.

Mount Kaimon (above) is very near the southernmost tip of Kyūshū. The region is famous for its hot springs (onsen) and subtropical climate, making it ideal for the cultivation of tobacco.

The Kintai Bridge at Iwakuni (left) is hardly suitable for walking across, but the design took into account the pleasing effect of the semicircular reflection in the water.

SATSUMA-JIRU

(*Miso*-flavored Vegetable Soup)

薩
摩
汁

INGREDIENTS (Serves 6)
1/2 medium daikon
1 carrot
1 cake konnyaku
2-3 cakes satsuma-age (deep-fried fish paste)
2 large satsuma imo (sweet red potatoes)
3 cups (24fl.oz) ichiban dashi
1/2 cup (6oz) shiro miso (white soybean paste)
1 green onion, sliced into thin rounds

(Illustration overleaf)

IN THIS THICK AND FILLING soup, lots of ingredients are cooked together. The cooking time is very brief, a typical Japanese characteristic.

Preparation

Cut the *daikon* and carrot into bite-sized pieces. Slice both the *konnyaku* and the *satsuma-age* cakes into six. Peel the *satsuma imo* and cut into slices 1/2in thick.

Bring 4 cups (32fl.oz) of water to the boil, drop in the *konnyaku* and allow the water to return to the boil, then drain and set the *konnyaku* aside.

Heat up the *ichiban dashi* in a large stewpot. Add the carrots and simmer for 3 minutes. Add the *daikon*, *konnyaku* and *satsuma imo* and cook another 3 minutes. Add the *satsuma-age* and cook another 2 minutes.

Dilute the *shiro miso* with some of the soup from the pan. When all the ingredients are cooked (tender but still crunchy), add the diluted *shiro-miso* and stir well. Do not boil. Sprinkle green onion over the top and then serve immediately.

HAKATA-MUSHI

(Steamed Ground Meat)

博
多
蒸
し

INGREDIENTS (Serves 6)
1 lb ground pork
2 tbsp flour
1 1/2 tsp salt
1 tbsp soysauce
3 eggs, lightly beaten
1 lb Chinese cabbage, boiled in salty water

DIPPING SAUCE:
2 cups (16fl.oz) ichiban dashi
2/3 tsp salt
2 tsp soysauce
1 tbsp cornstarch

WHEREVER WE FIND PORK in Japanese cuisine, we can suspect that Chinese influence is present. While the Japanese often grind fish and chicken, ground pork is definitely exotic — and the result is that this dish has a familiar sort of taste for foreigners. *Hakata-mushi* is served as a standard *mushimono* in a Japanese meal; it also makes an excellent canapé in the European style.

Preparation

In a bowl, mix the meat, flour, salt, soysauce, and a third of the beaten egg. You will need a 6in mold to form this mixture into an oblong. Line the bottom of the mold with a third of the Chinese cabbage leaves, and pour half of the remaining beaten egg over them.

On top of this, place 1/2in layer of ground meat. Cover with another third of the cabbage leaves and top that with another 1/2in meat layer. Pour the remainder of the egg over the top of the final meat layer, and top with the remainder of the cabbage leaves. Press down gently on the molded mixture to help it settle, then cover the mold with aluminum foil.

Put some water in a steamer and bring to a vigorous boil; place the mold in the steamer and steam for about 15 minutes, with the top tightly closed.

To make the dipping sauce: bring the *dashi* to the boil and add the salt and soysauce. Allow the mixture to return to the boil and add the cornstarch, stirring gently and constantly so that the mixture thickens. Allow to cool.

Unmold the *hakata-mushi* and allow it to cool to room temperature. Then cut it into 1½in squares and serve. Give each person a small dish of dipping sauce.

FUKI NO TOSA-NI

(*Fuki* Simmered in Clear Soup)

IN THIS DISH, the delicate sauce brings out the natural flavor of the *fuki* (coltsfoot), a stalky vegetable that resembles celery.

Preparation

Clean the *fuki* and strip off any leaves. Boil plenty of water in a large saucepan and add a pinch of salt (1 tbsp salt to 5 cups/40fl.oz of water). Slide the *fuki* stems into the boiling water, the bottom (thick) end first, and boil from 4 to 7 minutes, depending on the thickness of the *fuki*. Drain and quickly place in a bowl of cold water. In the water, peel the stems from the bottom end and drain. Cut into 2in sticks.

Put the *fuki* sticks and *ichiban dashi* together in a saucepan and bring the mixture to the boil. Add the sugar, *mirin* and soysauce and simmer for about 10 minutes, until the soup has reduced to half. Take the saucepan away from the heat and leave until the mixture has cooled down.

Place equal portions of the *fuki* into each serving dish and pour some of the juice into each bowl. Serve cold, garnished with bonito flakes.

路
ノ
土
佐
煮

INGREDIENTS (Serves 4)
4 *fuki* stems
pinch of salt
2 cups (16fl.oz) *ichiban dashi*
1 tbsp sugar
2 tbsp *mirin*
2 tbsp soysauce
bonito flakes

(*Illustration overleaf*)

■ SATSUMA-JIRU (page 126)
Miso-flavoured vegetable soup
Garnish: *green onion*

■ FUKI NO TOSA-NI (page 127)
Simmered coltsfoot
Garnish: *bonito flakes*

TAKENOKO NO TOSA-NI

(Shikoku Bamboo Shoots)

INGREDIENTS (Serves 4)
2 bamboo shoots (total of 1
   lb), trimmed and boiled
1½ cups (12fl.oz) ichiban
   dashi
1 tbsp mirin
2 tbsp soysauce
½ cup (1oz) dried bonito
   flakes (hana katsuo)

(Illustration overleaf)

THE TRADITIONAL Tosa seasoning touch — bonito flakes — is here applied to fresh, boiled bamboo shoots. For directions on selection, washing and boiling, see the basic recipe for boiled bamboo shoots (page 78).

You can substitute canned shoots, but it is far better if you can find fresh ones.

Preparation

Drain the bamboo shoots and cut them into ¼in wide wedge sections, lengthwise. The natural serration which occurs on the sections resembles comb-teeth.

Wash the little 'combs' carefully to free them of the small bits of white residue that may be clinging to them.

Combine the *dashi, mirin* and soysauce in a saucepan. Add the bamboo shoots and simmer, covered with an *otoshi-buta*, for about 15 minutes over moderate heat. Sprinkle half of the bonito flakes over the shoots and the simmering liquid. Remove from the heat and let the mixture stand until it has cooled to room temperature.

You now have a choice as to how you wish to serve the bamboo shoots. You can either serve them dry, having removed them from their liquid and rolled them in the remaining bonito flakes, or you can serve them in their simmering liquid. For the latter method, remove the bamboo shoots to a serving bowl or individual dishes with chopsticks or a fork. Strain the liquid through cheesecloth and discard the bonito flakes. Spoon some of the liquid over each serving of bamboo shoots, and scatter the remaining, fresh bonito flakes on top.

KAREI NITSUKE

(Simmered Flounder)

INGREDIENTS (Serves 2)
2 fresh flounder (karei)
7 tbsp sake
7 tbsp mirin
¾ cup (6fl.oz) dashi
7½ tbsp soysauce
a pinch of sugar
4 shishito (small green
   peppers)
⅛ daikon, peeled and cut
   into large chunks

(Illustration overleaf)

THE JAPANESE FLOUNDER (*karei*) is found at its best in the coastal waters of North Kyūshū and the entrance to the Inland Sea. This dish is quite delicious when served chilled — the simmering broth jells, and the whole thing becomes a pleasant summer main dish.

Preparation

Scale, gut and wash the fish, rinsing thoroughly. Do not remove their heads and tails (see instructions for cleaning flatfish, page 31). Make three parallel diagonal cuts on the top side of the flatfish. The cuts should be no deeper than about ¼in. These will enable the simmering liquid to penetrate the fish thoroughly.

In *sake* simmering, the alcohol in the rice wine is burnt off. Mix the *sake* and *mirin* together in a medium saucepan and heat slightly. Ignite the alcohol fumes with a kitchen match, and gently agitate the sauce to allow the vapors to be burnt off.

Stir the *dashi*, soysauce and sugar into the wine. Bring to the boil. Place the fish in the sauce, dark-skin-side-up. Place an *otoshi-buta* over the fish.

Continue cooking over a high heat, for about 10 minutes. In most simmered dishes, the liquid is not allowed to boil so rapidly — but in the case of the *karei*, fast cooking helps maintain tenderness. Using an *otoshi-buta* helps to maintain even heat and enables the seasonings to penetrate thoroughly.

To serve, remove the *otoshi-buta* and carefully lift out the fish with a wide spatula. With a flounder of approximately ½ lb, one whole fish can be served to each person. If the fish is very large, cut it on the diagonal into about 3in portions. If a whole fish is served, be sure to point its head toward the left, so that the traditional 'good side' is up. Garnish with *daikon*, cooked until just tender and cut into strips, and *shishito*, and spoon a bit of the simmering liquid over each fish.

SHIITAKE KARA-NI

(Simmered Mushrooms)

THE SHIITAKE MUSHROOM is used throughout Japanese cuisine in every part of the country. But every Japanese knows that the best *shiitake* of all come from Kyūshū. In this dish, the mushrooms spend quite a long time immersed — they cook until their liquid is nearly gone and they are heartily seasoned with soysauce and *sake*.

INGREDIENTS (Serves 6)
7 oz *shiitake mushrooms*, wiped and trimmed
½ cup (4fl.oz) *sake*
½ cup (4fl.oz) *soysauce*

Preparation
Slice the mushrooms into strips about ⅛in wide and set aside.

Mix the *sake* and soysauce in a saucepan (do not heat yet). Add the sliced mushrooms and cover with an *otoshi-buta*. Simmer over a very low heat until the simmering liquid is almost gone, stirring occasionally. Allow to cool to room temperature.

Shiitake kara-ni is quite pungent and is best enjoyed as a side dish with white rice. It is also quite good as a chilled 'relish' or 'chutney' — it keeps for a long time if covered and refrigerated.

■ TAKENOKO NO TOSA-NI (page 130)
Bamboo shoots rolled in bonito flakes
Garnish: *sansho leaf*

■ <u>KAREI NITSUKE</u> (page 130)
Simmered flounder
Garnish: <u>*shishito*</u> *peppers and* <u>*daikon*</u> *strips*

KAKUNI

(Nagasaki Braised Pork)

INGREDIENTS (Serves 6)
2¹/₂ lb raw slab of bacon
vegetable oil
2¹/₂ cups (20fl.oz) rice-
  washing water (the water
  in which a fine powder
  from washing rice remains
  in solution)
2 knobs fresh ginger (about
  3in), crushed
3¹/₂ cups (28fl.oz) niban
  dashi
1 cup (8fl.oz) sake
6 tbsp sugar
6 tbsp soysauce
6 tbsp mirin
12 pearl onions

STOCK FOR VEGETABLES:
2 tbsp soysauce
2 tbsp mirin
1¹/₄ cups (10fl.oz) niban
  dashi

GARNISH:
12 pearl onions
18 snow peas

角
煮

DURING THE LONG REIGN of the Tokugawa shogunate, Nagasaki was the only port in the nation open to foreign commerce. Dutch traders were relegated to a tiny man-made island in the harbor; but the other foreign group, the Chinese, had their own quarter in the city itself. Although eventually the Dutch were able to influence Japanese culture in surprising ways, the Chinese community was more visible and vital. One of their legacies to the Nagasaki area was an interesting hybrid cuisine called *shippoku* that combines elements of Chinese and Japanese cooking. This pork dish is typical of the more elaborate sort of *shippoku* dish. Typically, it might be served with a simple *consommé* and *sashimi*.

This dish takes nearly two days to prepare and cook, so plan accordingly.

Preparation

On the first day, cut the pork into cooking pieces of about 1 × 2¹/₂in and sauté in a small amount of oil, taking care to brown all sides. Drain the pork into a colander and discard the excess oil. Wipe the pan clean.

In a large saucepan, pour enough water to fill it three-quarters of the way to the top. Add the rice-washing water, crushed ginger, and pork.

Lower an *otoshi-buta* over the mixture and simmer over the lowest heat possible, for 5 to 6 hours. Keep the meat covered with liquid, adding water if too much boils away. Drain through a colander and discard everything but the pork. Rinse the pork thoroughly under cold water to remove the white residue from the rice-washing water.

Simmer the pork, in enough water to cover, for another 30 or 40 minutes, to eliminate the odor of the rice-washing water. Rinse and refrigerate the pork.

On the second day, remove the pork from the refrigerator and allow it to return to room temperature. Combine 3¹/₂ cups (28fl.oz) *niban dashi*, 1 cup (8fl.oz) *sake*, 6 tbsp sugar, 6 tbsp soysauce and 6 tbsp *mirin*, in a large saucepan. Add the pork and bring to a rapid boil. Reduce the heat, cover the mixture with an *otoshi-buta*, and simmer for 30 to 40 minutes.

Prepare the stock for the vegetables — combine the soysauce, *mirin* and *dashi*. Peel the onions and boil them in enough salted water to cover, until the onions have become translucent. Rinse in cold water to arrest cooking. Place three-quarters of the stock into a saucepan and add the onions. Simmer the onions uncovered for 2 to 3 minutes. Then discard the liquid.

Boil the snow peas in enough lightly salted water to cover, for 2 to 3 minutes then rinse them in cold running water. Place the remaining quarter of the vegetable stock in a small saucepan and simmer the snow peas until they are heated through. Drain, and discard the liquid.

Serve one or two pieces of pork, garnished with two onions and three snow peas to each person.

TORI CHIKUZEN-NI

(Fukuoka Chicken)

CHIKUZEN IS THE NAME of the ancient province (today's Fukuoka Prefecture) in the north of Kyūshū. The proximity of this region to Korea and the rest of the mainland may account for the fact that this dish is faintly Chinese — it employs stir-frying, a rare technique in Japanese cuisine.

Preparation

Cut the chicken in ¾in cubes. Choose decorative cuts for the mushrooms, bamboo shoots, burdock and carrots (see page 32 for instructions on cutting vegetables) — the sections should be about 1½in long. Cut the *konnyaku* into 1½in pieces.

Boil each vegetable in enough lightly salted water to cover. In general, you should boil just until the vegetable's color has been freshened. After boiling, always rinse thoroughly under cold running tap-water. Although boiling is not strictly required for this dish, it is highly recommended for freshening both color and flavor.

Place a small amount of vegetable oil — between 1 and 2 tbsp — in a sturdy, heavy-bottomed saucepan. Be careful not to use too much oil; the ingredients should absorb nearly all of it by the time the simmering stock is added. Turn the heat to high and add the chicken. Then add the *konnyaku*, mushrooms, carrot, bamboo shoot, and burdock in that order. Stir-fry for about 3 minutes, until lightly done. Make sure that the oil coats each piece of food evenly.

Pour the *dashi* over the mixture and allow it to come to the boil. Add the sugar and the two soysauces, stir, and lower the heat to bring the mixture to a simmer. Lower your *otoshi-buta* over the simmering mixture and simmer for about 15 minutes, or until the amount has been reduced by one-third.

Add the boiled snow peas and mix, just prior to serving. Serve hot or at room temperature in individual bowls.

INGREDIENTS (Serves 6)
1 lb chicken, boned, with skin
  attached
6 fresh shiitake mushrooms,
  wiped clean
4in section of bamboo shoot,
  washed thoroughly
1 burdock root (gobō),
  medium-size, washed and
  scraped
2 medium-size carrots,
  washed and peeled
1 cake konnyaku (gelatinous
  root)
vegetable oil
1 cup (8fl.oz) niban dashi
2 tbsp sugar
3 tbsp light soysauce
2 tbsp dark soysauce
2oz snow peas (boiled)

■ <u>TEMPURA</u> (page 138)
  Shrimp, cod and *shiitake* mushroom *tempura*
  Garnish: *shishito peppers and grated ginger*
  on grated <u>daikon</u>

TEMPURA

INGREDIENTS (Serves 6)
1 lb raw shrimp, shucked and
deveined
2 green peppers
1 carrot
1 small eggplant (1/2lb)
1 medium sweet potato
6 white mushrooms (or
shiitake mushrooms)
6in piece raw squid
2 medium onions
vegetable oil

BATTER:
2 egg yolks
2 cups (16fl.oz) ice-water
2 cups (7oz) sifted all-
purpose flour

3/4 cup (3oz) all-purpose
flour

DIPPING SAUCE:
1 cup (8fl.oz) ichiban dashi
3 tbsp light soysauce
1 tbsp mirin
1 tbsp sugar
1/4cup (1oz) grated daikon
(white radish)
2 tsp fresh ginger, peeled and
grated

(Illustration previous page)

TEMPURA is one of the most familiar of all Japanese dishes, both at home and abroad. It is a technique for coating nearly everything with a light and lacy coat of batter that turns milky white or golden when deep-fried, depending upon the amount of egg in the batter.

This familiar national dish finds its place in the Kyūshū section because it was almost certainly invented in Nagasaki — not, however, by the Japanese. Between 1543 and 1634 Nagasaki was the center of a great community of missionaries and traders from Spain and Portugal. Like homesick foreigners everywhere, they did their best to cook foods from their home countries, and batter-coated and deep-fried shrimp happened to be a particular favorite throughout southern Europe. The name *tempura* (from Latin *tempora* meaning 'times') recalls the *Quattuor Tempora* ('The Four Times', or 'Ember Days') — feast days on the Roman Catholic calendar when seafood, especially shrimp, was eaten. When the dish became Japanized, however, its range was extended almost infinitely. Beef, pork and chicken are almost the only things not prepared as *tempura*, and these all have separate deep-frying traditions anyway. Favorite foods for *tempura* treatment include shrimp, eggplant, snow peas, sweet potato slices, mushrooms of all sorts, carrots, peppers, squid, small whole fish, lotus root, small trefoil leaves and okra (ladies' fingers).

The crucial factor in making good *tempura* is the batter. This should be so light and subtly-flavored that it could almost pass as an elaborate seasoning. There are only three ingredients in it, and all three have an equally important part to play in producing the sort of *tempura* you want. Egg yolk is beaten very slightly first, then some ice-water is added. Finally, finely sifted flour is added. Reducing the egg amount will make the finished batter coating lighter in color; more egg will make a golden *tempura* (the former is preferred in Ōsaka, the latter in Tokyo). The amount of ice-water determines the relative heaviness or lightness of the batter — for very light, lacy *tempura*, add more water. The flour should be barely mixed with the other ingredients — to achieve real lightness, the batter should look lumpy, undermixed and unfinished-looking, and it must always be prepared just before you use it; thoroughly mixed, silky batter that has been allowed to 'set' and settle simply will not produce good *tempura*.

Here is a recipe for you to use as a guide; once you have mastered the techniques of batter-making and deep-frying, use your imagination in deciding what to treat *tempura*-style.

Preparation

Score the shrimp a few times crosswise on the underside, to prevent them curling-up during deep-frying. Tap the back of each shrimp with the back-edge of your knife.

Core and remove the seeds from the peppers; trim and slice into strips. Wash and scrape the carrot; cut into strips about 1½in long and ⅛in wide.

Peel the eggplant, leaving ½in strips of the peel intact here and there for decorative effect. Cut in half lengthwise, then into slices ¼in thick. Wash the slices and pat them dry with kitchen towelling.

Peel the sweet potato and slice it crosswise into ½in rounds. Cut the mushrooms in half. Cut the flattened piece of squid into ½in squares.

Cut the onions in half. Push toothpicks into the onion at ½in intervals, in a straight line. Then slice the onions midway between the toothpicks. The toothpicks will hold the layers of onion together in each of the sliced sections.

Pour the vegetable oil into a large pot or electric skillet. The oil should be heated to about 350°F (mark 4).

Make the batter in two batches. Place one egg yolk into a mixing bowl; add one cup (8fl.oz) of ice-water and mix with *only* one or two strokes. Then add 1 cup (3½oz) of flour, and mix as before, with only a *few* brief strokes. Prepare the second batch of batter when the first is used up. The batter should be lumpy, with some undissolved flour visible.

Check the oil for heat: drop a bit of batter into the oil; if the batter sinks slightly beneath the surface, then comes right back up surrounded by little bubbles, your oil is ready.

Dip each item into flour first — this ensures that each ingredient is perfectly dry and that the batter will adhere well. Then dip in the batter, shake a little to remove any excess batter, and slide into the oil. Fry each piece for about 3 minutes, or until lightly golden. In order to maintain the oil temperature, make sure that no more than a third of the surface of the oil is occupied by bubbling pieces of frying food.

Remove the pieces from the oil and place on an absorbent paper towel to drain for a few seconds. Then transfer to your guests' plates, which should also be lined with attractive absorbent paper. The best arrangement is to reproduce the Japanese *tempura* bar — the cook at one end of the table or behind a kitchen counter, and the guests seated within easy reach. You may also keep *tempura* warm in a 250°F (mark ½) oven, but do not leave them for any longer than about 5 minutes.

To make the dipping sauce: combine the *dashi*, soysauce, *mirin* and sugar in a small saucepan. Heat until the sugar has dissolved and serve warm, with a little grated *daikon* and ginger on the side for each guest to combine with the dipping sauce according to taste. Dip the *tempura* in the sauce and eat.

■ <u>TORI-MIZUTAKI</u> (page 143)
Chicken one-pot with a dipping sauce
Garnishes: *<u>momiji-oroshi</u> and chopped green onion*

KAKI-NABE

(Oyster Stew)

INGREDIENTS (Serves 6)
2 lb large oysters, opened
1 tbsp salt
3 Japanese-style long onions
(naganegi) or substitute 4
leeks
2 bunches of enokitake
mushrooms (small
Japanese tightly curled
mushrooms)
6 shiitake mushrooms
¼ head Chinese cabbage
3 bunches of edible
chrysanthemum leaves
(shungiku)
6 tbsp white miso
6 tbsp red miso
1 tbsp mirin
½ cup (4fl.oz) dashi (cooled
to room temperature)
1 piece konbu (kelp) — about
3 × 5in
4 cups (32fl.oz) warm
ichiban dashi
6 medium eggs

牡
蠣
鍋

ASK A CULINARY-MINDED JAPANESE about Hiroshima, and he will immediately reply with one word: oysters. The oyster beds off the shores of this city supply all of Japan. Almost certainly, the Hiroshima-ite will serve his out-of-town guests some sort of oyster dish — perhaps this cheerful one-pot. As we explore regional food, the one-pot will appear again and again as one of the favourite Japanese alternatives to the fancy food of the classical (Ōsaka-Kyōto) variety.

Preparation

The seafood and vegetables can be prepared a few hours ahead of cooking time, if you wish.

Fill a large bowl with warm water, add the oysters and 1 tbsp salt. Swish the oysters about in the salty water to whiten and clean them. Then discard the salt-water, remove the oysters, and rinse them thoroughly under very cold tap water. Drain and set aside.

Decide upon a decorative cut for the long onions — diagonal, perhaps, or *ran-giri* (see page 33) — and cut them into 1½in lengths.

Trim the roots from the *enokitake* mushrooms. With the *shiitake* mushrooms, either cut them in half across the caps, or make a decorative 'x' on the top of each mushroom cap.

Cut the cabbage into 1½in sections. Separate the chrysanthemum leaves into groups of equal size. Arrange all the vegetables on a large tray.

Mix the two varieties of *miso* (light and dark) together with a fork or chopsticks, then add the *mirin* and the ½ cup (4fl.oz) of cool *dashi* and blend very well. Spread this *miso*-paste on the inside walls of a casserole that can take direct flame or electric heat.

Take the sheet of *konbu* seaweed and place it at the bottom of the casserole — it will help flavor the stock. Then pour in the 4 cups (32fl.oz) of *dashi*.

If you have a portable heating unit, bring it to the table and place it in the center where all of your guests can reach it. Bring the *dashi* to a brisk boil as quickly as possible, then reduce the heat to medium. This is an ad-lib dish; using chopsticks, each person drops the ingredients of his/her choice into the simmering *dashi*, and scrapes some of the *miso* into the pot. Serve a little lightly beaten raw egg to each person as a dipping-sauce, if desired. Be careful not to overcook the oysters of *shiitake*.

The stew soon becomes fragrant with the *miso* and the other ingredients.

TORI-MIZUTAKI

(Chicken One-Pot)

WE CROSS THE STRAITS OF SHIMONOSEKI to North Kyūshū for this dish — to the Hakata region, where Kyūshū's biggest city, Fukuoka lies. This is Hakata's favorite chicken stew; it is very mildly flavored — just a hint of seaweed — and becomes pungent when it is dipped in *ponzu* (citrus-soy sauce).

Preparation

Boil the chicken in 2 cups (16fl.oz) of boiling salted water — for about 10 seconds, or until the chicken turns lightly white. Drain and rinse under cold tap water to arrest cooking.

Cut off the base of the cabbage, discard the upper stem area, and wash thoroughly. Bring 2 cups (16fl.oz) of salted water to the boil, and drop the cabbage in. Boil for about 1 minute, or until the leaves wilt; then cover the saucepan and boil for an additional 1 minute. Drain and run the cabbage under cold tap water to arrest cooking.

Place the cabbage leaves one on top of another in the middle of a *sudare* (bamboo mat, see page 20) and roll them up as tightly as possible. Hold the roll for a few seconds, then unwrap the mat from the roll of cabbage. Slice the cabbage crosswise into rounds about 1in wide.

Boil the carrots in 1 cup (8fl.oz) of unsalted water: bring to the boil, drop in the carrots, allow the water to return to the boil, and drain. Rinse the carrots under cool running tap water.

Make an interesting arrangement of the chicken, cabbage rolls, carrots, *naganegi* strips, *tōfu*, mushrooms and chrysanthemum leaves on a large serving platter. The Japanese like to place the various ingredients in concentric rings.

Mix the soysauce and the citrus juice, and give each person some of the mixture in a little bowl; also place condiments of finely grated *daikon* spiked with hot red pepper ('red maple grate', page 82), and finely chopped green onion in separate small dishes, so that each person can mix them into the dipping sauce as desired.

In a large casserole, place the *konbu* square at the bottom and pour 4 cups (32fl.oz) of chicken stock over it. Bring the stock to a lively boil, then reduce to a medium heat. Each person chooses his or her own ingredients from the serving platter, and dips them into the bubbling pot. Food cooks for about 3 minutes, then the person removes it and drops it into the dipping sauce.

When all the ingredients have been cooked and consumed, it is customary to serve the broth — enriched as it now is with many good tastes — as a meal-ending soup course.

INGREDIENTS (Serves 6)
2 whole chicken breasts, boned and cubed (1in cubes)
salt
2 lb Chinese cabbage
4 large carrots, washed, scraped and cut decoratively (see page 36)
2 naganegi, cut diagonally into $^{1}/_{2}$in strips
2 cakes of tōfu, cubed (1in cubes)
6 dried shiitake mushrooms, soaked in water for about 30 minutes before use
12 small white mushrooms or 1 large bunch enokitake mushrooms, wiped and trimmed
$^{1}/_{2}$ bunch chrysanthemum leaves, washed and trimmed (substitute 12 sprigs watercress)

SAUCE AND GARNISH:
6 tbsp soysauce
6 tbsp lemon or lime juice
1in piece of daikon
1 dried hot red pepper
2 green onions, finely chopped or cut into tiny rounds

1 square konbu (dried kelp) — about 3 × 5in
4 cups (32fl.oz) chicken stock — fresh, if possible

(Illustration previous page)

YAKI-SHIITAKE PONZU-AE

(Broiled Mushroom Salad)

INGREDIENTS (Serves 4)
12 large shiitake mushrooms,
    wiped (not washed) and
    trimmed

PONZU SAUCE:
6 tbsp soysauce
6 tbsp lemon juice (or lime
    juice)
mirin
1 tbsp finely chopped green
    onion

(Illustration overleaf)

焼き椎耳咋ん酢合え

THIS IS ANOTHER DISH that allows the lowly but delicious *shiitake* mushroom to shine. It is rather unusual in that the 'salad' is served piping hot, in *ponzu* sauce (soy and citrus). The fact is that it is not easy to draw hard and fast lines between certain classes of Japanese foods. *Yaki-shiitake ponzu-ae* is technically an *aemono*, 'something put together', because it features a simple ingredient with a sauce added. But, if the *ponzu* sauce was to be served on the side, as an ad-lib dipping sauce, the dish would then fall within the *yakimono* ('broiled thing') category. The broiled eggplant (*nasu no an-kake*, page 106) is another such dish that just makes it into the capacious salad category.

Preparation

Salt-broil the mushrooms, by first salting them lightly and then placing the mushroom tops directly over a hot charcoal fire, on skewers (use bamboo skewers). Broil the stem side first, then the cap side, about 3 minutes per side. It is important not to overcook the *shiitake* mushrooms, as they will dry out easily.

Mix the soysauce and lemon or lime juice, and add a little splash of *mirin*. Stir well with a fork or chopstick. Add the finely chopped green onion.

Serve two mushroom tops to each diner, as soon as they come off the fire. Top each serving with a little *ponzu* and eat while very hot.

TOSA-ZU

(Shikoku Vinegar)

INGREDIENTS
Makes 1⅓ cups (10fl.oz)
1½ tbsp mirin
½ cup (4fl.oz) rice wine
    vinegar
2 tbsp soysauce
⅔ cup (6fl.oz) dashi
a little more than 1 cup
    (2oz) dried bonito flakes
    (hana-katsuo)

(Illustration overleaf)

土佐酢

BONITO MAKES ANOTHER appearance in this vinegar sauce, which can be used for nearly any *sunomono*.

Preparation

Mix the *mirin* and vinegar in a saucepan over a medium heat, then add the soysauce. The *dashi* should be blended next, but taste the mixture as you do so in order to achieve the strength and pungency you prefer. Bring to the boil and add the bonito flakes. Stir over the heat for 30 seconds or so, then strain and discard the bonito flakes. Allow to cool to room temperature. You can make larger quantities of *Tosa-zu*, if you wish, as it will keep indefinitely if refrigerated.

TAI MESHI

(Sea Bream Rice)

THE COASTAL WATERS of Kyūshū teem with sea bream, far and away the favorite Japanese fish — and the Inland Sea is even more famous for the delicacy. Sea bream (*tai*) is a holiday favorite because of a pun: *medetai* means 'felicitous, well-omened' — and every *tai* is a *medetai*. On holidays, the fish is presented in the *sugata-yaki* or *o-kashira-tsuki* style — with head and tail attached, and the solemn *tai* eye staring right up at the person eating it. This dish is an informal version of the holiday treat, cooked *en casserole*. If you have a *donabe* (see page 21), use it for this dish; otherwise, any large casserole that will stand direct flame will do.

Preparation

You can broil the sea bream a long time before assembling the other casserole ingredients, if you wish.

Scale and gut the fish, but leave the head and tail intact (see page 30). Skewer, using the *uneri-gushi* technique (see page 58), so that the fish looks as if it is actively swimming. Salt lightly and broil over hot coals for about 8 minutes on each side.

Wash the rice several times, until the washing water is only very slightly cloudy, then drain.

Put the rice in the casserole and add a few drops of *mirin*, the soysauce, 1 tsp salt and the *dashi*. Top the rice with the broiled fish — the fish should be facing toward the left.

Cover with a lid and cook as for rice. Bring to a high boil until froth appears under the lid, then reduce to a very low heat until the regular, low, bubbling sound begins to sound dry and sparse. Remove from the heat and allow to rest and steam for about 20 minutes.

The sea bream deliciously flavors its rice 'bed', and the rice-making steam keeps the broiled fish deliciously moist.

Before you feed your guests, show them the handsome fish, whole, and then flake the fish off the bones, adding rice as you serve.

INGREDIENTS (Serves 3)
1 whole seam bream
  (substitute sea bass, sea
  trout, or salmon)
salt
2½ cups (17fl.oz) Japanese-
  style short-grain rice
few drops mirin
2 tbsp soysauce
3⅓ cups (27fl.oz) ichiban
  dashi

■ <u>YAKI-SHIITAKE PONZU-AE</u> (page 144)
Broiled mushroom salad
Garnishes: *chopped green onion and <u>momiji-oroshi</u>*

■ TOSA-ZU (page 144)
Shikoku vinegar

THE KANSAI

*T*hrough the centuries the Kansai Plain played an important role in the emerging 'empire' of Japan. For 1,100 years — between 500 and 1600 — it was the home of Japanese power and culture. Except for the brief attempt in the thirteenth century to make the little seaside hamlet of Kamakura a new Kyōto in the East, the great old political, religious and trading centers of the Kansai retained their amazing magnetism, educating the tastes and attracting the patronage of successive military groups, long after the Imperial Court had lost almost all political power.

THE JAPANESE STATE first crystallized in the Kansai as a confederation of chieftains under one paramount head. For many generations, Japanese ritual law decreed that the chieftain's palace had to be destroyed after his death, and the rude 'capital' moved. It was not until mature Chinese institutions began to spread in Japan that the idea of a permanent capital took hold. After a few false starts, the little city of Nara rose up in southern Kansai, an earnest, miniature version of the Chinese capital. Through the eighth century, Nara thrived and a handsome Buddhist culture was created. When the capital moved to Heian-kyō (later Kyōto), classical Japanese civilization entered its mature phase. A brilliant court culture, witty, poetry- and music-loving and addicted to fine clothes, it set the standards for Japanese elegance.

Although the Heian-era court was not known for its gourmandising, what the aristocrats ate was the finest and freshest that their country had to offer. As a sort of nexus of sea, mountain and fertile lands, the Kansai is ideally situated to support fine eating. Succulent *matsutake* mushrooms, high quality tea, an enormous variety of seafood and wondrous fruit and vegetables are just some of the products supplied by the Inland Sea and the mountains, the dry fields, and the low land of the Kansai.

Kyōto's traditions of elegance and understatement created a cuisine that was more refined than exuberant. Two influences — the tea ceremony and Zen Buddhism — combined to inspire not only Kyōto food but the whole concept of Japanese *haute cuisine*. The important idea that fancy food should be served in many small portions, beautifully arranged, came from the practice of the tea-masters, who served a frugal and elegant meal before preparing the tea itself. Likewise, seasonality and pristine freshness — values fundamental to Japanese cuisine — found their finest expression in tea-taste cooking (*kaiseki ryōri* in Japanese). The Zen temples of the region made another distinctive contribution to Kyōto taste with *shōjin* cooking, a vegetarian cuisine that makes great use of *tōfu* and simple fresh vegetables.

Kansai culture and life would be rich enough if Kyōto was the only great city in the region, but, with a fine sense of balance, history allowed an anti-Kyōto to grow up at the eastern end of the Inland Sea. The great city of Ōsaka thrived in medieval times, after military houses had displaced the Imperial court from power. Feudal armies needed provisions and weapons; the merchants and

The Kinkakuji (Golden Pavilion) was first built in 1394. It is one of the finest examples of Muromachi period architecture, and each floor represents a different style. For over 1,000 years, to 1868, Kyōto was the capital city and the center of art and religion. In 1950 the Pavilion was destroyed by an arsonist, and the present building is an exact copy, carried out in 1955. Tōfu (inset) is a curd made from the soybean; its small cubes have the consistency of set custard, and it is a great source of protein.

Ōsaka Castle (above) was first built in 1586 by the great Toyotomi Hideyoshi, whose plans for unification after the ravages of civil war during the 16th century prepared the way for the feudal period, the expulsion of the missionaries and the eventual closure of Japan from the rest of the world in 1639 for over 200 years. The present castle is a reconstruction of the original, carried out in 1931.

financiers of Ōsaka provided both. By the late sixteenth century, Ōsaka was the undisputed commercial capital of Japan. The townsmen were proud, wealthy and pleasure-loving *bourgeois* who enjoyed both cultivating and parodying the elegance of old Kyōto. New schools of art, literature and performance, such as woodblock prints and the *bunraku* puppet plays grew up and flourished, as did the gay, licentious life-style of the licensed brothel quarters, heralding a new era in Japanese culture.

Ōsaka passed the mantle of cultural leadership to Edo (Tokyo) in the mid-eighteenth century, but the special qualities of the city remained — Ōsaka citizens are still renowned for their commercial sharpness, their taste for down-to-earth pleasures, and, above all, their love for good, tasty food. The Kyōto-ite, say the Japanese, is a fool for fine cloth — but the Ōsaka man is a fool for great food. Together, the two great Kansai cities define the extremes of Japanese cuisine: elegance and refinement on one hand and a downright, uncomplicated pleasure in convivial good eating on the other.

Near Kyōto, small boats brave the rapids to Arashiyama (left). A 2¹/2-mile avenue of torii (entrance gates) leads to the Fushimi-Inari shrine *(below). Bright red maple trees surround the temple of Jingo ji (bottom), whose belfry carries a large bell cast in 875.*

MISO-ZŌNI

(*Mochi* Stew with *Miso*)

INGREDIENTS (Serves 4)
3½ cups (28fl.oz) ichiban
   dashi
¼ tsp salt
1 tsp light soysauce
6in section of daikon (white
   radish)
4in section of a medium
   carrot
1 wedge of bamboo shoot,
   boiled
2½ tbsp light miso
1 small bunch of edible
   chrysanthemum leaves
   (shungiku) or other greens
4 mochi cakes (glutinous rice
   'taffy')

(Illustration overleaf)

味
噌
雑
煮

THIS IS A KANSAI variation on the favorite holiday soup (see page 47) that includes two mainstays of western Japanese cooking: light soysauce and light, or white, *miso*.

Preparation

Heat the *dashi* in a large pot, and add the salt and soysauce. Peel the *daikon* and cut it in half lengthwise, then slice it into ½in half-rounds (*hangetsu-giri* cut, page 33). Wash and peel the carrot, then slice it into ¼in rounds. Rinse the bamboo shoot section carefully — there will probably be some white residue sticking to the serrated 'comb' part of the shoot section. Slice the shoot into ¼in wedges.

Cook the *daikon*, carrot and bamboo in the seasoned stock over a moderate heat, for about 10 minutes. Place the *miso* in a small bowl, and spoon a little of the simmering stock into the bowl. Mix thoroughly, softening the *miso*. Add all the *miso* to the stock and stir well to blend it. Remove the pot from the heat.

Boil the greens in enough salted water to cover for about 20 seconds. Drain and rinse the greens under cold running water to arrest cooking.

Place the *mochi* cakes in enough water to cover and soak for about 5 minutes. Then bring to a low boil and cook for a minute or so. Drain.

Place one *mochi* cake in the bottom of each person's bowl. Around it make an attractive arrangement of the greens and the other vegetables. Heat the soup to a near-boil, then fill each bowl with soup, about two-thirds full. Eat with a spoon and chopsticks.

YŪAN-YAKI

(Soy-*Sake* Marinade Grill)

INGREDIENTS (Serves 4)
½ lb salmon (or 1 large
   mackerel, filleted)
1 tbsp citron (or lemon) juice
2 tbsp soysauce
2 tbsp mirin
2 tbsp sake

(Illustration overleaf)

幽
庵
焼
き

MOST JAPANESE BROILING involves some combination of salting and dipping — the salting brings out natural juices, and the dipping sauce adds piquancy. This variation on the standard *yakimono* uses a soy and *sake* marinade to fulfill both functions.

Preparation

Quarter the salmon lengthwise and take off all of the skin except a narrow strip in the center of the fish. Marinate the salmon for 2 to 3 hours in the mixture of citron juice, soysauce, *mirin*, and *sake*. Turn over the fish from time to time to marinate evenly.

Skewer each salmon piece fanwise on three to four skewers. Broil the skin-side first for about 2 minutes over a very hot charcoal fire. Broil the other side for about 1 minute. Remove the skewers from the salmon and cut into pieces 2in long.

Place the salmon on a *shiso* leaf and serve garnished with a piece of *kamaboko* (fish paste cake) or just a wedge of lemon.

YAWATA-MAKI

(Burdock and Beef Rolls)

THIS IS A MODERN VARIATION on an old Kansai favorite, named after a region near Kyōto where the burdock was especially fine and famous. The modern element is, of course, beef. The traditional *Yawata-maki* is made with fillets of eel. This is a time-consuming dish, but one well worth the extra labor involved.

Preparation

Cut the burdock root into thin lengthwise strips. All the strips should be of approximately equal width, to ensure even cooking. In a large saucepan, bring 1 quart (32fl.oz) of water to the boil. Add ½ tbsp of vinegar to the water. Add the burdock strips and boil until soft. Remove the burdock from the saucepan and plunge into cold water until cool.

Combine the ingredients for the burdock marinade — the light soysauce, *dashi*, salt and *mirin* — in a large bowl and marinate the cooled burdock strips for about 4 hours.

To make the rolls: Ask your butcher to cut the beef into paper-thin slices, then cut these slices into 2 × 4in strips. Take a third of these strips and lay them next to each other, with their edges overlapping so that they form a 'sheet'. Press down gently on the overlapping sections, to help the meat stick together. Put a cluster of about eight burdock strips at the edge of this meat 'sheet', and carefully roll the burdock up in the meat. Tie the roll in three or four places with white cotton string.

Mix the ingredients together for the beef marinade: the soysauce, *sake* and *mirin*. Put the marinade into a wide, flat pan and add the beef-and-burdock rolls. Marinate for 1 hour, turning the rolls several times. After marinating, reserve the liquid for basting.

To broil: Skewer the rolls fanwise; two rolls will fit on one 'fan'. Broil over hot charcoal for 6 minutes in total, turning once. Watch the meat closely and broil until medium- to well-done, depending on your preference. Baste once or twice during broiling.

Twist the skewers a few times during the broiling, to loosen and to make removal easier. Remove the skewers, cut the strings that bind the meat, and slice the rolls into ½in lengths.

INGREDIENTS (Serves 4)
BURDOCK AND MARINADE:
4 medium-size burdock
    (gobō) roots
½ tbsp vinegar
2 tbsp soysauce
1⅔ cup (14fl.oz) ichiban
    dashi
½ tsp salt
3 tbsp mirin

BEEF AND MARINADE:
1½ lb prime beef, sliced
    paper-thin
6 tbsp soysauce
3 tbsp sake
6 tbsp mirin

(Illustration overleaf)

八幡巻き

■ <u>MISO-ZONI</u> (page 152)
Rice cake stew
Garnish: <u>*harusame*</u>

■ <u>YUAN-YAKI</u> (page 152)
Salmon in a soy-<u>*sake-mirin*</u>-lemon marinade
Garnishes: <u>*shiso* leaves and a <u>*kamaboko*</u> (fish paste) slice</u>
(Illustration opposite top)

■ <u>YAWATA-MAKI</u> (page 153)
Burdock and beef rolls
Garnishes: *mayonnaise, sliced cucumber, lettuce and tomatoes*
(Illustration opposite bottom)

TŌFU DENGAKU

(*Tofu* on a Stick)

INGREDIENTS

WHITE MISO TOPPING:
3/4 cup (6oz) white miso
2 egg yolks
2 tbsp sugar
2 tbsp sake
2 tbsp mirin
7 tbsp niban dashi
ginger juice

GREEN MISO TOPPING:
ingredients for white miso (above)
pinch of tea powder (for a darker effect, substitute a drop of green coloring)

RED MISO TOPPING:
1/2 cup (4oz) red miso
3 tbsp white miso
2 egg yolks
2 tbsp sake
2 tbsp mirin
2 tbsp sugar
7 tbsp niban dashi

2 cakes tōfu

(Illustration overleaf)

豆
腐
田
楽

DENGAKU IS NOT a culinary word. It refers to a medieval open-air public entertainment held on temple grounds — a sort of vaudeville that was earthy, funny, and very popular. From the Kyōto temple-entertainment scene emerged two of Japan's great contributions to world theatre: the Nō and the Kabuki, and from the holiday-like atmosphere of these performances came this dish — a genuine medieval 'fast-food' that was later served along Japan's post-roads. The idea is simplicity itself: broiled *tōfu* cakes on a little stick, covered on one side with a delicious *miso*-mixture.

It is traditional to cook and eat *tōfu dengaku* on small two-pronged skewers that resemble forks. They might be available in Japanese goods shops, but if not, two short skewers of bamboo will do very well. 'Cotton' *tōfu* should be used; although it is firmer than 'silk' *tōfu*, it is still very fragile and should be handled with great care when skewered.

To make toppings: You will need a double boiler for the toppings. In the top of the boiler, combine the white *miso*, egg yolks, sugar, *sake*, and *mirin*. Bring some water to the boil in the bottom boiler, place the top over the bottom, and stir in the *dashi*. Just before you spread the sauce on the *tōfu*, add a little ginger juice.

To make green *miso* topping, add a pinch of tea powder (for a subtle effect) or a drop of coloring when you stir in the *dashi*.

To make red *miso* topping, follow the procedure above, beginning with the two types of *miso* mixed together in the top of the double boiler.

To prepare the tōfu: Use 2 full cakes of *tōfu*. Remove them from the water-pack in which they are sold and wrap each cake in a clean, dry kitchen towel. Place a plate over each cake and leave them to stand for about 1 hour. This presses excess water out of the *tōfu* and makes it easier to broil.

Cut the *tōfu* into small sections, measuring about 3/8 × 3/4 × 2in. Insert a two-pronged skewer or two single bamboo skewers into each piece, and broil over hot charcoal for about 3 minutes on each side. The outside surface will become speckled brown — do not overcook.

Spread one side of each of the *tōfu* cakes with the *miso* topping of your choice. Use garnishes to complement the colors of the toppings. Return the *dengaku* to the broiler — *miso*-side-up — and broil for about 1 minute more, until the topping is heated through. Serve two or three of the skewered pieces to each person.

AMADAI WAKASA-YAKI

(Broiled Tilefish)

IN THE PAST, tilefish had to be salted for the journey from Wakasa Bay across the Tamba Mountains to the Kyōto markets. The salting is still done today in the kitchen, no longer as a necessity, but as an integral part of the flavoring process.

Preparation

Using the *sanmai oroshi* technique, cut the fish into two full fillets. You do not need to skin or scale the fish. Salt both sides of the fillets and leave to stand for 24 hours. Wash the fillets thoroughly and pat dry with kitchen towelling. Pass a long metal skewer through the front part of each fillet, tie cords onto the skewer on either side of the fillets and hang this arrangement in a cool, dry place for another 24-hour period (you can reduce the time if necessary).

Cut each fillet crosswise into three pieces. Skewer on paired skewers and broil, skin-side-first, for 5 minutes. Mix the light soysauce and *sake*.

Turn the fish and broil the flesh side for 3 minutes. Baste both sides with the soy-and-*sake* mixture, and broil each side briefly until the sauce dries. Repeat two or more times on both sides.

Twist the skewers in place a few times to make them easier to remove. Pull out the skewers and serve the fillet pieces, skin-side-up on a bed of *shiso* leaves, garnished with sections of lemon and a few ginger shoots.

甘鯛わかさ焼き

INGREDIENTS (Serves 6)
1 red tilefish
salt
½ cup (4fl.oz) light soysauce
½ cup (4fl.oz) sake
shiso (if unobtainable,
*   substitute lettuce)*
2 lemons
8 pink pickled ginger roots

(Illustration page 162)

■ TŌFU DENGAKU (page 156)
Tōfu on a stick
Garnishes: *white sesame seeds (red topping)*
citrus rind (white topping)
sansho leaf (green topping)

TAI NO TAMBA-MUSHI

(Steamed Bream)

INGREDIENTS (Serves 4)
1 sea bream about 1¹/₂ lb
12 chestnuts, shucked and
    peeled
salt
1 piece of konbu seaweed,
    about 4 × 6in
4 tbsp sake

SAUCE:
2 cups (16fl.oz) ichiban
    dashi
1 tbsp light soysauce
¹/₂ tsp salt
4 tbsp sake
2 tbsp cornstarch
fresh ginger juice or lemon
    juice

(Illustration overleaf)

鯛
の
丹
波
蒸
し

THIS SUCCULENT DISH, which contains the delicate, white-fleshed sea bream, takes it name from the Tamba Mountains which enclose the northern edge of the Kansai Plain. The chestnuts are the products of the Tamba forests.

Preparation

Scale the fish, gut and rinse. Using the sanmai-oroshi technique (see page 30) make boneless fillets (use tweezers to remove the small bones). Do not skin the fillets. Salt on both sides, wrap in a moist cloth, and refrigerate for about 1 hour. Then wash the fillets thoroughly under cold running water and pat dry with kitchen towelling.

Slice the fillets on the diagonal into 2in wide serving pieces. Make two or three shallow cuts crosswise on each piece to help slow down shrinkage during cooking.

Cut the piece of konbu into four sections, after wiping with a damp cloth. Place one of the konbu pieces in the bottom of each person's bowl. Place a piece of fish on top of each piece (the konbu will help flavor the fish during steaming).

Add about a tbsp of sake to each portion, then wrap each dish tightly with aluminum foil. Steam in a standard steamer for 15 minutes, over a high heat.

Heat the dashi in a small saucepan. Add the soysauce, salt and sake. Bring to a low boil and simmer. Add 2 tsp water to the cornstarch and stir into a paste. Add this cornstarch mixture to the simmering sauce, stirring until the sauce thickens. Stir in a little ginger or lemon juice.

Remove the bowls of fish from the steamer and top each with a little of the sauce.

NASU NO RIKYŪ-NI

(Eggplant in Sesame and Bean Sauce)

INGREDIENTS (Serves 4)
³/₄ lb eggplant
vegetable oil
¹/₃ cup (3fl.oz) ichiban dashi
3 tbsp dark miso
1¹/₂ tbsp sake
2 tbsp sugar
2 tsp white sesame seeds

茄
の
離
宮
煮

THIS LIGHT, DELICIOUS eggplant dish owes its special quality to a combination of sesame and miso. It is named after Sen no Rikyū, perhaps the most famous of all the masters of the tea ceremony, who explored the use of sesame in tea-ceremony cuisine. This dish embodied all the restraint and elegance of tea-taste cooking.

Preparation

Peel the eggplant, remove the stem, and quarter. Cut the eggplant into cubes (about ¹/₂in). Put a little vegetable oil into a skillet and sauté the eggplant cubes over a medium-high heat, until they are translucent. Add the *dashi* and simmer over a very low heat for 5 minutes, using an *otoshi-buta*.

In another pan, combine the *miso, sake*, and sugar, and heat until the sugar dissolves, stirring occasionally. Add this thick sauce to the simmered eggplant and cook over a low heat for 2 more minutes.

Dry-roast the sesame seeds in a small pan. Allow them to become golden, but be careful not to overcook them. When they have been toasted, remove them to a *suribachi* or mortar, and grind them lightly, releasing their flavor. Stir about three-quarters of the seeds into the simmering eggplant mixture. Then remove the mixture from the heat.

Garnish the eggplant with the remaining sesame seeds and serve warm or at room temperature.

KAMO YOSHINO-NI

(Duck in Thickened Sauce)

THIS RECIPE is for duck prepared as a traditional Japanese *nimono*. Characteristic of Kyōto cooking is the use of starch (*kuzu* or cornstarch) to thicken the sauce.

Preparation

Slice the duck breasts on the diagonal into long, thin pieces. Salt lightly.

In a medium-sized saucepan, bring 2 cups (16fl.oz) of water to the boil, and add the duck slices. Allow the water to return to the boil, and remove the duck slices; set aside.

In another medium-sized saucepan, combine the *sake* and *dashi* and bring to the boil. Add the sugar, soysauce and salt. Then add the duck and the grated ginger and reduce the heat to bring the mixture to a simmer. Cook uncovered for 3 to 4 minutes.

Remove the duck pieces from the simmering liquid and set aside for a moment. Mix the cornstarch or *kuzu* starch with 1 tbsp of water and add to the simmering liquid. Still simmering gently, stir until the starch is thoroughly blended and the sauce thickens.

Serve the duck slices, topping portions with the thickened simmering liquid.

INGREDIENTS (Serves 6)
1 whole duck breast, with
    skin attached, boned
1 tbsp cornstarch or kuzu
    starch
salt
¼ cup (2fl.oz) sake
1 cup (8fl.oz) niban dashi
1 tsp sugar
½ tsp soysauce
½ tsp salt
2 tbsp grated, fresh ginger
    root

鴨
吉
野
煮

■ <u>AMADAI WAKASA-YAKI</u> (page 157)
Broiled tilefish
Garnish: *pickled ginger*

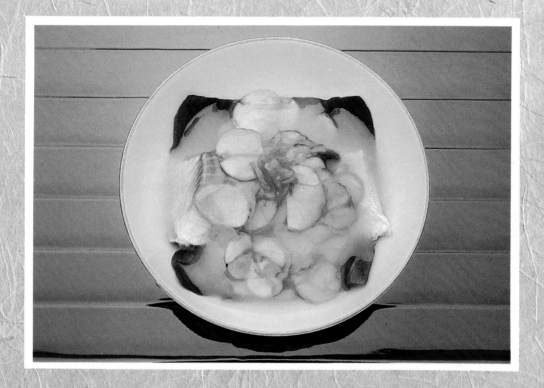

■ <u>TAI NO TAMBA-MUSHI</u> (page 160)
Steamed bream
Garnish: *finely sliced red pepper*

YUDŌFU

(Boiled *Tōfu*)

INGREDIENTS (Serves 4)

DIPPING SAUCE:
½ cup (4fl.oz) soysauce
2 tbsp mirin
1 tbsp dried bonito flakes
*   (hana-katsuo)*

GARNISH:
4 green onions
1 sheet toasted nori seaweed,
*   cut into fine shreds*
1 tbsp grated fresh ginger
½ cup (1oz) dried bonito
*   flakes*

4in square of konbu (kelp)
4 cakes of tōfu

(Illustration overleaf)

THIS SIMPLE DISH epitomizes the Zen influence in Kyōto cooking. Many of the temples in and around the old city serve their characteristic vegetarian dishes to the general public and a number of 'secular' restaurants also prepare temple specialties. Because it can be used in so many ways and served in so many forms, *tōfu* is an important part of vegetarian cooking in the Far East. Real devotees insist that it is never more delicious than when it is simply boiled and enjoyed with dipping sauce. In fact, in this dish, the *tōfu* is not even boiled — just heated through in simmering water.

Preparation

The 'cooking' of this dish is so simple that it is the dipping sauce and garnishes that require the most attention. Combine the soysauce, *mirin* and dried bonito flakes in a small saucepan and bring to the boil. Then remove from the heat.

Slice the green onions into very thin rounds. Give each person a portion of dipping sauce, with little rounds of *nori* seaweed shreds, ginger, green onions and bonito flakes on the side. Each person can then add garnishes to the dipping sauce according to taste.

Wipe the *konbu* seaweed with a damp cloth, and score it a few times with a knife, to help bring out the flavor.

Carefully cut each *tōfu* cake into sixths. Pour 6 cups (48fl.oz) of cold water into an electric skillet or large saucepan over a heating unit. Add the *konbu* seaweed and the *tōfu* pieces. Bring the water to a simmer over a medium heat. Make sure the heat is not too high or the *tōfu* will become dry and unpalatable.

As soon as the *tōfu* is heated through, gently lift the pieces out with a slotted spoon and serve, dividing the *tōfu* evenly among everyone.

UDON SUKI

(Noodle *Sukiyaki*)

THIS DISH is very popular in Ōsaka, and it is perfect for convivial eating. A variety of ingredients are arranged over a bed of cooked noodles on a platter. As the meal progresses, with everyone helping to cook the ingredients, the noodles are uncovered. They are eaten last of all with the flavorsome broth.

Preparation

Cook the dried noodles in vigorously boiling water for about 10 minutes, drain and wash under cold running water to remove surface starch. Do not overcook, as they will be cooked again in the broth later. Arrange the noodles on a platter.

Chop the chicken breast into bite-sized pieces. Drop the Chinese cabbage leaves in a large pot of salted, boiling water, and boil for about 2 to 4 minutes, until tender. Drain in a colander and place the cabbage under cold, running water. Drain again. Boil the spinach in a similar manner, until the leaves are limp and dark (about 2 minutes).

Place a sixth of the boiled spinach on a Chinese cabbage leaf. Roll from the top of the leaf downwards. Cut the cabbage roll into two. Repeat for the rest of the spinach and cabbage.

Cut both the *tōfu* cakes into six cubes. Make an egg roll (see page 62) and cut into six pieces. Slice the *konnyaku* cake into six.

Wipe and trim the *shiitake* mushrooms. Cut the *naganegi* diagonally into thin pieces. Soak the *harusame* in warm water for 5 minutes.

Place all the prepared ingredients — the chicken, spinach and cabbage rolls, *tōfu*, egg roll, *konnyaku*, *shiitake* mushrooms, *naganegi*, shrimp, *harusame*, *enokidake* mushrooms, gingko nuts, chrysanthemum leaves and salmon, turbot and squid slices — on top of the noodles and garnish with flower-cut carrots (see page 36) and *fu*.

Mix together the ingredients for the dipping sauce: the soysauce, grated *daikon*, finely chopped green onion and lemon juice, and pour into little bowls.

Boil the chicken stock in a saucepan or flameproof casserole on a table cooking unit. People pick up whatever they like, cook it in the broth, dip it into the sauce and eat.

After all the other ingredients are eaten, cook the noodles on their own in the remaining broth. Add more stock if needed. Season well with salt, pepper and soysauce. Divide the noodles into six and eat with the broth.

INGREDIENTS (Serves 6)
1 lb dried udon noodles
1 whole chicken breast
6 large Chinese cabbage
  leaves
1/2 lb spinach
2 cakes tōfu
1 egg roll (see page 62)
1 cake konnyaku
6 fresh shiitake mushrooms
1 naganegi (or a bunch of
  thick green onions)
2oz harusame
6 large shrimp, shucked and
  deveined (or 2 large
  shrimp and 2 crab claws)
1/2 lb young chrysanthemum
  leaves
1 bunch of enokidake
  mushrooms
6 gingko nuts
4 slices salmon
4 slices turbot fillets
4 slices squid
'flower' cut carrots
decorative fu (wheat gluten
  cake)

FOR DIPPING SAUCE:
6 tbsp soysauce
6 tbsp grated daikon
2 tbsp finely chopped green
  onion
6 tbsp lemon juice

FOR BROTH:
5 cups chicken stock
pinch of salt and pepper
3 tbsp soysauce

(Illustration overleaf)

■ YUDŌFU (page 164)
Boiled *tōfu* with a *shiitake* mushroom
Garnishes: *grated ginger, shredded nori, finely chopped green onion and bonito flakes*

166

■ <u>UDON SUKI</u> (page 165)
Noodle <u>*sukiyaki*</u>

SU-UDON

(White Noodles in Broth)

INGREDIENTS (Serves 6)
14oz package of udon
1 tbsp salt
6 cups (48fl.oz) ichiban
    dashi
1 tbsp sugar
1 tbsp soysauce
2½ tsp salt
2 green onions, trimmed and
    cut into small rounds

すうどん

THERE ARE COUNTLESS noodle shops in Japan offering a variety of noodles in a myriad of different ways. Fat white *udon* noodles in steaming broth are a symbol of the Kansai — and especially of the hearty eating habits of Ōsaka people. The true noodle connoisseur, like the real *aficionado* of Italian pasta, likes to eat noodles accompanied only by a very simple broth. This recipe is the equivalent of *linguine al burro* — 'simple udon'.

Preparation

Bring 2 quarts (64fl.oz) of water to the boil in a large saucepan. Add the noodles and let the water return to the boil. Boil briskly, stirring, until the noodles are quite soft (about 20 minutes). Add 1 tbsp of salt and cover the saucepan. Remove from the heat and let the noodles stand for 5 minutes.

Drain the noodles and, using a colander, run cold water through them for another 5 minutes, to arrest cooking. Drain thoroughly and set aside; allow the noodles to 'warm up' to room temperature.

In a medium-sized saucepan, combine the *dashi*, sugar, soysauce and 2½ tsp of salt. Stir well and bring to the boil over a high heat. Add the noodles and allow the broth to return to the boil. Boil for a few minutes until the noodles are heated through; then serve. Using chopsticks or a fork, first serve the noodles, then add the broth. Garnish each bowl with a scattering of green onion.

For a richer dish, try 'Moon Viewing' (*Tsukimi*) udon. After serving the *udon*, break one egg into each bowl. In place of the green onion, scatter flakes of crumbled dried *nori* seaweed. The hot broth cooks the egg, and the seaweed adds an appetizing tang.

TORI NAMBA UDON

(Chicken-Onion Noodles)

INGREDIENTS
14oz package of udon
salt
6 cups (48fl.oz) ichiban
    dashi
1 tbsp sugar
1 tbsp soysauce
1 lb chicken meat, boned and
    skinned
6-8 green onions

鶏南蛮うどん

HERE IS ANOTHER *udon* variation, named after the Namba district of Ōsaka, once famous for its wild onions. Namba is entirely urbanized now, a part of the great, bustling Kansai metropolis — but the several dishes that have Namba in their names all commemorate the past by featuring green onions.

Preparation

Prepare the noodles and broth according to the recipe for *su-udon* (see above). However, before you add the noodles to the broth, cut the chicken meat into ¾in squares and onions into 1in lengths. Add the chicken to the broth, and simmer for about 10 minutes. Add the green onion and simmer for another 1 minute. Add the noodles and heat them through. Garnish with green onion and serve.

KITSUNE UDON

('Fox' Noodles)

FRIED TŌFU joins *udon* in this dish, named after the tricky and intrepid fox of Japanese folklore. Tradition has it that foxes are inordinately fond of fried *tōfu*.

Preparation

Wrap the *tōfu* cake in dry kitchen towelling and weight it with a plate. Allow it to stand for 30 minutes, drain, and pat dry. Slice the *tōfu* into ¼in pieces.

Bring 1½in of oil to a medium heat (350°F/mark 4) in a heavy bottomed skillet. Fry six of the *tōfu* slices at a time, turning them once with a slotted spoon or chopsticks. When the slices are golden brown, remove them from the oil and drain well on absorbent paper. Dip each *tōfu* slice into a bowl of warm water briefly to clear the oil from the surface. Drain once again on absorbent towelling.

Use a large saucepan to bring 2 quarts (64fl.oz) of water to the boil. Add the noodles and allow to return to the boil. Boil briskly, stirring, until the noodles are quite soft (about 20 minutes). Add 1 tbsp of salt and cover the saucepan. Remove from the heat and let the noodles stand for 5 minutes.

Drain the noodles and, using a colander, run cold water through them for another 5 minutes, to arrest cooking. Drain thoroughly and set aside; allow the noodles to 'warm up' to room temperature.

In a medium saucepan, combine 1 cup (8fl.oz) of *niban dashi*, 2 tbsp of sugar and 1 tbsp of soysauce. Stirring, bring to the boil over a high heat. Add a little salt and place the *tōfu* slices in the liquid. Allow to return to the boil and cook for about 6 minutes, or until the liquid is reduced by two-thirds. Remove from the heat and set aside.

Combine 6 cups (48fl.oz) of *ichiban dashi*, 1 tbsp sugar, 1 tbsp soysauce and 2½ tsp salt. Stir, bring to the boil, and add the noodles. Allow to return to the boil and serve. Top each bowl with pieces of *tōfu* and decorate with garnishes of your choice.

INGREDIENTS (Serves 6)
6oz cake of tōfu (use 'cotton' tōfu)
vegetable oil
14oz package of udon
salt
1 cup (8fl.oz) niban dashi
2 tbsp sugar
1 tbsp soysauce
6 cups (48fl.oz) ichiban dashi
1 tbsp sugar
1 tbsp soysauce

(Illustration overleaf)

■ KITSUNE UDON (page 169)
Udon noodles and fried *tōfu*
Garnishes: *sliced kamaboko (fish paste), sheet of nori
seaweed, trefoil and citrus rind*

■ SABA-ZUSHI (page 172)
Mackerel _sushi_ with _nori_ seaweed
Garnishes: *pickled ginger and bamboo leaves*

SABA-ZUSHI

(Mackerel *Sushi*)

INGREDIENTS (Serves 8)
2 whole mackerel
4 tbsp kosher salt
⅔ cup (5fl.oz) rice wine
vinegar
5 tbsp sugar
2 tbsp light soysauce
2 cups (14oz) uncooked rice
¼ cup (2fl.oz) sushi-su
(seasoned vinegar for
sushi)
several slices of red pickled
ginger (beni shōga)

(Illustration previous page)

SUSHI MAY BE MOST familiar to you in its Tokyo form: little rice ovals topped with slices of raw fish — the whole delicious snack prepared before your eyes. This is *nigiri-zushi*, and it is dealt with in the Tokyo chapter (page 196). *Sushi* actually stands for many different types of vinegared rice dish. The recipe here requires quite a lot of preparation, but when you eat it you are tasting one of the oldest variations of this versatile technique, and a typical type of Kansai *sushi*. The origins of *sushi* are not entirely clear, but it seems that the Japanese first used vinegared rice, along with salt, as a preservative for fish.

Preparation

Clean, scale and fillet the two mackerel, using the *sanmai-oroshi* technique to produce four boneless fillets. Salt the fillets on both sides and let them rest in a covered, non-metallic container for 4 hours in a cool, dry place. Pour the liquid off, remove the small bones with tweezers and rinse the fillets completely in cool running water, and pat dry.

Combine ⅔ cup (5fl.oz) vinegar, the sugar and soysauce in a small saucepan and bring to the boil. Stir to make certain all the sugar is dissolved, then remove from the heat and allow the mixture to cool to room temperature.

Place the fillets, skin-side-up, in a glass or ceramic dish. Pour the marinade over the fillets, and let them marinate for 3 hours, unrefrigerated but in a cool place.

Cook the rice according to the standard procedure for Japanese rice (see page 94). Add the *sushi-su* to the rice and mix thoroughly, fanning the rice as your work in the vinegar. Moisten your hands, and use them to shape eight rice-balls. Press them firmly together when

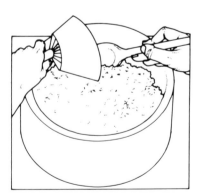

1. *Cool the hot rice with a fan while you mix in the sushi-su. When the vinegar has been mixed in, shape the rice into balls.*

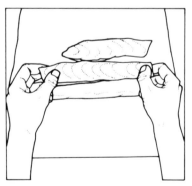

2. *Slice the marinated fillet into two. Place the thinner piece of fish beside the thicker part to form an oblong shape.*

3. *Cover a sudare mat with a damp napkin. Place a fillet pair on the napkin and on top of this, place two rice balls.*

formed; cover with a damp cloth to preserve freshness while you continue preparing the fish.

Remove the fillets from the marinade and peel off the transparent outer skin. Place the fillets skin-side-down and slice each fillet horizontally, into two pieces. Place the smaller, thinner part of the fillet beside the larger part to form an oblong shape. This will form the loaf top.

Next shape the oblong rice-and-mackerel loaves. It you have a *sudare* mat, place it on your work surface and cover it witha damp linen napkin (you can also use a mould designed specifically for this recipe). Put an oblong-shaped fillet pair skin-side-down on the napkin. On top of this place two of the rice balls.

Now gently spread the rice-balls over the surface of the fillets; you are aiming to make a single squared-off rice-and-fish block. You can lift up part of the *sudare* and cloth to provide an edge to work against. Bring the *sudare* and cloth all the way over the rice-and-fish block while shaping. You can also use the cloth alone, gently twisting the ends to make the loaf firmer and more compact.

Gently wrap your squared-off loaf in aluminum foil, and place a trimmed piece of cardboard on the top and bottom. Secure with rubber bands and weight with an approximately 1 lb plate or book. Repeat this process for the three other fillet pairs and the other rice balls, making four loaves in total.

Allow the loaves to rest, secured and weighted, for 2 hours or longer. Do not refrigerate.

Remove the loaves from their wrappings and, with a very sharp knife, cut each loaf into five or six pieces. Moisten the blade each time you cut. Serve each loaf 're-assembled' and garnished with a piece of red ginger.

A slight variation on this recipe is to roll the loaves with a piece of *nori* sandwiched between the rice balls.

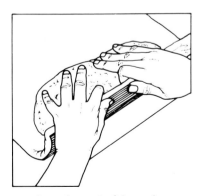

4. Lift up the end of the sudare and cloth to provide a supporting edge while you spread the rice balls evenly over the fillet pair.

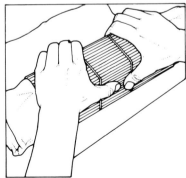

5. Then, fold the sudare and cloth over the fish and rice combination in order to pack the loaf firmly. The mackerel fillets are now on top.

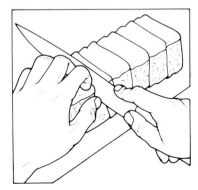

6. Having secured and weighted the loaf (minimum 2 hours), remove the wrappings and use a sharp knife to slice the loaf.

TOKYO AND THE KANTŌ

*F*rom North Kyūshū to Tokyo there stretches an almost unbroken belt of highly developed commercial, industrial and residential land; and the Kantō Plain, which lies at the north-eastern end of this 700-mile corridor, is the most highly developed part of the whole region. Historically, the plain was unimportant until medieval times when the warrior (*samurai*) class rose up and established power there. A few centuries later, it became the site for the future capital of Japan. Today, the Kantō is Japan's center of population, the hub of its commerce and its window on the rest of the world. If the Kansai represents old Japan at her finest, then the Kantō is the birthplace and the showplace of modern Japan.

ONE IN EVERY THREE JAPANESE lives in the Kantō Plain, an area of some 2,700 square miles giving the plain as a whole an average population density of 300 people per square mile. In metropolitan Tokyo, however, the figure is more like 2,000 people per square mile, and feels like it. But Tokyo is more than a great hive of population. Far more than London or Paris, it is the center of national communication, transportation, heavy industry, banking, publishing, and mass media — virtually everything that can be centralized is centralized in this great city.

Tokyo arose because of a conscious political decision on the part of Japan's great unifier, Tokugawa Ieyasu (1542-1616). For many centuries the Kantō was the cradle of the *samurai* class, the ambitious warriors who managed to wrest real power from the Imperial Court as early as 1180. Nonetheless, the Kansai still remained the center of power and culture.

Ieyasu, who was determined to change the violent course of

Modern high-rise office blocks dominate the skyline of Shinjuki Park (below) in north-west Tokyo. Although Tokyo is densely populated, the many parks give a feeling of space and a refuge from the bustle of city life. The Ginza (right) is one of the most famous shopping areas in the world. The names means silver (gin) place (-za), since the national mint once stood on the site.

Nigiri-zushi (inset) is a Tokyo specialty and there are countless sushi bars and restaurants in the city selling this delicious fish and rice 'sandwich'.

The Nijubashi (above) is the bridge that leads into the grounds of the Imperial palace, in the heart of Tokyo. The Japanese royal family can be traced back to the first century AD, and had divine status until 1946 when Emperor Hirohito, immediately after World War II, officially renounced the Imperial line's claim to divinity.

Japanese history, deliberately shifted the center of the Japanese world to the east, to an obscure fishing village called Edo. Here he built a capital, and a social order, that was intended to last indefinitely. Paradoxically, the authoritarian Tokugawa order gave birth to one of the most vital and lively cities of the entire eighteenth century. Edo inherited the hedonistic merchant culture of Ōsaka (Kansai influence, even upon popular culture, remained strong) and took it to great heights of sophistication and opulence. The gorgeous, elaborate popular theatre called *kabuki* and the full-color woodblock print (*nishiki-e*) are typical products of the ripest age of Edo culture, a culture that the Tokugawa authorities periodically attempted to suppress.

When Japan set out on the path of modernity and imperial glory after 1868, Edo (renamed Tokyo, and made the official seat of both imperial and bureaucratic authority) was a ready-made metropolis; in 30 years, it became a modern city, strung with electric wires, crowded with factories and dotted with public buildings in high Victorian style. Since the 1890s, Tokyo has been Japan's most cosmopolitan city as well as her most important one.

Tokyo eating is a mosaic of the major culinary traditions around the world. French cuisine is an old and honoured heritage; there are fine Italian and German restaurants, at least one first-rate New York style kosher delicatessen, Indian and Indonesian eating places in abundance, and every imaginable size, shape and variety of Japanese restaurant.

It is to be expected in a city where there is such a richness of choice, that Tokyo food *per se* tends to be a bit overshadowed. The culinary heritage of the Kantō is not as rich as that of western Japan and Tokyo's successive transformations have made traditions sometimes hard to trace. In other words, Tokyo cuisine is as various and complicated as the modern history of Japan itself, and the selection of recipes here reflects this variety. They include specialties that every Japanese associates with the national capital, along with familiar favorites that made their first appearance in the city; there are also recipes for delicious 'fast foods' that Tokyoites eat on the go, as well as for dishes that reflect urban, not rural, Japanese eating.

The Tokyo Tower (below) rises to a height of 1,100 ft and carries telecommunication equipment — a reminder that Japan leads the world in the electronics industry.

The Daibutsu (Great Buddha) at Kamakura (below) is second only in size to the Great Buddha at Nara.

The main gate to the Asakusa-Kannon Temple (right), is set in the heart of the entertainment quarter.

Kabuki Theatre (bottom) combines dance and song, and dates from the 17th century. All the roles are taken by male actors.

The Iris Garden (above) at the Mei ji Shrine, is dedicated to Emperor Mei ji, who ended Japan's 200 years of isolation and ushered in the great Mei ji Reformation (1867-1912).

Tokyo citizens admire the cherry blossom at Kitano-maru Park (left). Spring blossoms and fall tints play an important part in Japanese sensibility.

UNAGI KABAYAKI

(Broiled Eel)

INGREDIENTS (Serves 4)
2 eels, filleted, with skin
    attached
3 tbsp soysauce
3 tbsp sake
3 tbsp sugar
sansho (Japanese pepper)

(Illustration overleaf)

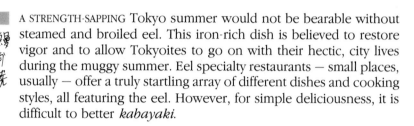

A STRENGTH-SAPPING Tokyo summer would not be bearable without steamed and broiled eel. This iron-rich dish is believed to restore vigor and to allow Tokyoites to go on with their hectic, city lives during the muggy summer. Eel specialty restaurants — small places, usually — offer a truly startling array of different dishes and cooking styles, all featuring the eel. However, for simple deliciousness, it is difficult to better *kabayaki*.

Preparation

Cut the eel fillets into six or eight pieces measuring 4 to 5in apiece. Using three bamboo skewers, skewer two of the eel pieces crosswise. Repeat for the remaining eel slices.

Put the skewers into a steamer, taking care that the eel itself does not touch the sides or bottom of the steamer. For the soft type of *kabayaki* favored in Tokyo, steam for 15 to 20 minutes. Remove the skewers from the steamer.

Broil the eel over moderately hot charcoal — do not place the skewers too near the charcoal. Allow the skin to brown slightly — it should take about 5 or 6 minutes. Twirl the skewers occasionally so that they can be removed easily without damaging the fish.

Mix the soysauce, *sake* and sugar. Use a pastry brush to coat both sides of the eel fillets generously with the mixture. Broil for 8 to 10 additional minutes, glazing with the sauce constantly and turning the fillets frequently. Remove from the heat and pull the skewers out gently. Serve on top of white rice, and season with a sprinkle of *sansho*.

YAKITORI

(Skewered Chicken)

HERE IS A DELICIOUS marinated chicken dish that, if not indigenous to Tokyo, is most delicious there. Like so much of the best food in the capital city, *yakitori* is a food-stand and tiny-restaurant specialty; a skewer of chicken is a common after-work snack. A bottle or mug of fine Japanese beer is the perfect accompaniment. Countless harried office workers relax over *yakitori* and beer every day, before facing the long journey home.

Preparation

In a mixing bowl, combine the *sake*, sugar and soysauce. Mix well and add the sliced ginger. Add the chicken livers and marinate for 6 hours at room temperature. Remove the livers from the marinade and cut them in half. Reserve the marinade.

Cut the chicken breasts into 1in cubes, and the green onions into 1½in sections.

Skewer four half-livers onto each of four skewers. Skewer four pieces of chicken, alternately with three green onion sections, on each of eight skewers.

Broil the skewered livers about 3in away from hot charcoal, for about 4 minutes. Glaze the livers with *teriyaki* sauce, turn, and broil the other side for 4 to 5 minutes. Set aside.

Glaze the chicken-breast-and-green-onion skewers with *teriyaki* sauce and broil for 2 minutes on each side. Repeat the glazing and broiling.

Serve two chicken-and-green-onion-skewers and one liver-skewer to each person, moistening the food with a little of the marinade. Top with sprinkles of *sansho* pepper.

INGREDIENTS (Serves 4)
3 tbsp sake
2 tsp sugar
1 tbsp soysauce
1in piece of fresh ginger,
    peeled and thinly-sliced
8 chicken livers, fat trimmed
    away
2 whole chicken breasts,
    boned
8 green onions
1½ cups (12fl.oz) teriyaki
    sauce
sansho (Japanese pepper)

(Illustration overleaf)

■ <u>UNAGI KABAYAKI</u> (page 180)
  Broiled eel, served on top of rice

■ <u>YAKITORI</u> (page 181)
Skewered chicken
Garnish: *parsley*

TEPPAN YAKI

(Mixed Grill)

INGREDIENTS (Serves 4)
4 small boneless 6oz rib
    steaks
2 green peppers
4oz fresh bean sprouts
2in piece of daikon (white
    radish)
1 dried red pepper
½ lemon or lime
6 tbsp soysauce
3 tbsp ichiban dashi
beef suet or vegetable oil

(Illustration overleaf)

鉄
板
焼
き

THE TEPPAN STYLE of cooking steak is a postwar addition to urban Japanese eating. Originally conceived as a concession to foreign tastes, it has now caught on among the Japanese. Restaurants which specialize in this dish either turn their entire counter into a griddle, or place individual griddles on each table so that chefs can broil the food right in front of the customers. In your home, you can use an electric griddle, electric skillet or a skillet over a heating unit.

A wide variety of ingredients can be cooked *teppan* style, including chicken, beef and many types of seafood and vegetables.

Preparation

Trim any excess fat from the steaks. Slice the green peppers in half, remove the seeds, then cut the peppers into eighths, lengthwise. Soak the bean sprouts in cold water for about 30 seconds, then drain and pat dry.

Using a chopstick, poke four or five evenly-spaced holes into one end of the *daikon* section. Fill these holes with strips of hot peppers (after removing the seeds from the peppers) and grate the *daikon* and pepper into a cheesecloth. Drain the excess moisture and place the mound of condiment (called *momiji-oroshi*, 'red-maple-grate') in a shallow bowl. On a separate small plate, place a row of lemon or lime slices. Give each person a small bowl and pour into it a bit of soysauce and a few drops of *dashi*.

Having prepared the dipping sauce and condiments, you are ready to start cooking the steak and vegetables. In a heavy, large skillet, melt some suet (or oil). Sear the steak on both sides, then slice into ½in thick strips as it cooks. Divide the steak strips among everybody, then put the green peppers into the skillet. Stir-fry for about 2 minutes, then divide and serve. Stir-fry the bean sprouts for no longer than 1 minute and serve.

Everyone can squeeze a little lemon or lime juice on the food, add *momiji-oroshi* to the soy-and-dashi dipping sauce, dip, and eat.

TORI MUSHIYAKI

(Steamed Chicken)

MUSHIYAKI (steam-broiling) is a technique that is not particularly familiar to Westerners who eat Japanese food, but its simplicity and goodness recommend it highly. *Mushiyaki* means sealing moist ingredients in something (a clay pot, in the cooking style called *hōrakuyaki*; or, as here, in little packets of aluminum foil) and placing the lot upon hot coals. The natural moisture of the ingredients, held in by the container, steam-cooks them.

Preparation

Cut the boned chicken into 1in cubes. Sprinkle the mushrooms and chicken with *sake*, and let them stand briefly. Sprinkle salt on the mushrooms, chicken and gingko nuts.

Make two square sheets of aluminum foil, about 1ft in size, and place half of the ingredients in each. Wrap the sheets into two tidy and airtight packages.

Put the packages directly on a hot charcoal broiler and broil for 4 minutes on each side (turn with long chopsticks). Then carefully remove the food from the packages, or simply split the packages open.

Mix the soysauce and lemon juice to make a dipping sauce; garnish with a lemon wedge if desired.

INGREDIENTS (Serves 2)
1 whole chicken breast, boned, with skin attached
6 matsutake mushrooms (drain if canned)
2 tsp sake
½ tsp salt
10 gingko nuts
soysauce and lemon juice in equal measure, for dipping

ODEN

(Hotchpotch)

THIS DISH is called *Kantō-daki*, 'Kantō stew', in western Japan. A favorite way for Tokyoites to warm up during the blustery, raw Kantō winter is to huddle around the mobile stand of an *oden*-man, eating this filling, fortifying hotchpotch.

Preparation

Bring 2 cups (16fl.oz) of water to the boil in a medium saucepan. Add the *konnyaku* and allow to return to the boil. Boil for 1 minute and drain.

In a skillet, heat 2in of vegetable oil to 350°F (mark 4), and fry the *tōfu* for 4 minutes, turning once. The *tōfu* should become a light golden brown. Drain on absorbent towelling and set aside.

In a large saucepan, combine the *dashi*, salt, sugar, soysauce and *sake*. Stir and bring to the boil. Add the *konnyaku* and *daikon*, reduce the heat, and simmer uncovered for 1½ hours. Add more stock if necessary to keep the ingredients covered. Add the potatoes, *kamaboko* slices, eggs and bamboo shoots. Simmer for 15 additional minutes.

Transfer the solid ingredients to a casserole and ladle the cooking liquid over them. Keep the casserole warm by placing it over an alcohol burner or other heating element at your table. Let everybody serve themselves from the common pot.

INGREDIENTS (Serves 6)
2 pieces konnyaku (gelatinous root)
vegetable oil
1 cake of tōfu, cut into equal sixths
4 cups (32fl.oz) niban dashi
1 tsp salt
1 tbsp sugar
1 tbsp soysauce
3 tbsp sake
6 slices of daikon, about ½in
6 small new potatoes, peeled
13oz can of kamaboko (fish cake), or fresh kamaboko, cut into 1in slices
6 hard-cooked eggs, shucked
3 bamboo shoots, cleaned, boiled and cut in half crosswise

■ TEPPAN YAKI (page 184)
Shrimp, salmon and cod fillets cooked on a griddle

186

■ EBI TEPPAN YAKI (page 184)
Shrimp cooked *'teppan'* style

TONKATSU

(Deep-Fried Pork Cutlet)

INGREDIENTS (Serves 4)
*4 slices pork loin or
  tenderloin,
  ¹/₂in thick*
salt
black pepper
flour
2 eggs, lightly beaten
*2 cups (4oz) dried bread
  crumbs*
vegetable oil
3in wedge of cabbage
¹/₂ lemon
ketchup
Worcestershire sauce
dark soysauce
mustard
sake

(Illustration overleaf)

TONKATSU is an interesting word, half-Japanese and half fragmented English. *Ton* is 'pig' or 'pork', while *katsu* is the Japanization of 'cutlet'. The dish itself is of European origin, and still very similar to breaded pork cutlet in the West. It is a phenomenally popular 'fast food' in Tokyo and other cities, a cheap and filling everyday treat.

Preparation

Score the edges of the cutlets in a few places to keep the edges from curling during the frying process. Salt and pepper both sides. Dredge in flour, dip into beaten egg and then coat both sides with breadcrumbs.

Fill a heavy pot with about 3in of vegetable oil and heat to 350°F (mark 4). Deep-fry one or two cutlets at a time, for 5 to 7 minutes, turning once or twice. Skim the oil to keep it clean and clear. Remove the cutlets and drain them for a few seconds on absorbent towelling.

Slice the pork on the diagonal into ³/₄in wide strips. Shred the cabbage and make four little 'beds' for the slices. 'Reassemble' each sliced cutlet on the cabbage (as if the cutlet was whole) and garnish with a lemon wedge.

Combine the ketchup, Worcestershire sauce, soy, mustard and *sake* to taste and put into individual bowls for a dipping sauce — or spoon some sauce directly on the cutlet slices.

SUKIYAKI

SUKIYAKI IS ALMOST as familiar as *tempura* in the West, and like *tempura*, it is a sort of European-Japanese hybrid. *Sukiyaki* began its career as a stylish way for Tokyoites to incorporate beef, the most Western of foods, into their culinary repertoire. The habitués of *sukiyaki* parlours in the late 1880s were the type of Japanese who wore bowler hats with their traditional robes and jackets, carried umbrellas, and fished gold watches out of their kimono sleeves to find out the time. Today, *sukiyaki* is a party food, and a great Japanese favorite.

Preparation

Ask your butcher to slice the beef into very thin, almost translucent pieces by using the ham slicer, or freeze the beef for 45 minutes and slice it yourself. Arrange on a platter and garnish the slices with a sprig of parsley.

Cut the *naganegi* or green onions on the diagonal into ½in sections. Drain the package of *shirataki* noodles and cut them into 6in lengths. Drain the *tōfu* cakes and cut both into sixths. Wash the cabbage, cut into 1in wedges, and dry with kitchen towelling. Rinse and trim the spinach leaves. Wipe the *shiitake* mushrooms and trim off the stems. Cut the caps in half if they are large. Slice the *konnyaku* cakes into 6 pieces. Arrange all the ingredients attractively on a large serving platter.

Give each person a bowl, and break an egg into each bowl. The egg is lightly beaten with chopsticks and used as a dipping sauce.

An electric skillet is ideal for *sukiyaki*. Bring it to the table (or bring a heating unit and a large regular skillet) and melt suet into it over a medium heat, moving the suet around on the surface with chopsticks to oil the pan. Place some of the beef and the onion into the pan. Sear the beef quickly on both sides. Discard the suet. Move the beef quickly to one side and add a little bit of each of the other ingredients. Season with some of the *dashi*, soysauce, *sake*, and sugar.

Each person helps him or herself to the cooked ingredients in the skillet, and dips them into the raw egg. As the food depletes, add some more fresh ingredients to the pan (beef first) and replenish the simmering liquids.

INGREDIENTS (Serves 6)

すき焼き

1½ lb beef round steak,
sliced paper-thin
1 sprig of parsley
2 naganegi (or a bunch of
large green onions)
1 package shirataki noodles,
soaked in warm water for
5 minutes
2 cakes tōfu
½ lb Chinese cabbage
4oz spinach
6 fresh shiitake mushrooms
(or ordinary mushrooms)
1 cake konnyaku
1 bunch enokitake
4oz cooked udon noodles
6 eggs
piece of beef suet
1 cup (8fl.oz) ichiban dashi
½ cup (4fl.oz) soysauce
3 tbsp sake
3 tbsp sugar

(Illustration overleaf)

■ <u>TONKATSU</u> (page 188)
Deep-fried pork cutlet
Garnishes: *tomatoes, cucumber, lemon slice, lettuce and mayonnaise*

■ <u>SUKIYAKI</u> (page 189)
Beef and vegetable one-pot

KATSUDON

(*Tonkatsu* Rice Bowl)

INGREDIENTS (Serves 4)

FOR TONKATSU:

4 slices pork loin, or
*   tenderloin,*
*   ¹/₂in thick*
salt
black pepper
flour
2 eggs, lightly beaten
2 cups (4oz) dried
*   breadcrumbs*
vegetable oil

small bunch trefoil
1 onion (small)
2¹/₂ cups (20fl.oz) niban
*   dashi*
7 tbsp mirin
5 tbsp soysauce
6 beaten eggs
8 cups (48fl.oz) hot rice,
*   cooked Japanese style (for*
*   instructions, see page 94)*

(Illustration overleaf)

ANOTHER POPULAR WAY to eat *tonkatsu* is on top of a good bowlful of rice, with egg and onion. This is one of the most popular *domburi* — hot, boiled rice dishes with toppings, covered in a sauce — that serve beautifully as fast, simple lunches for hard-working Japanese urbanites.

Preparation

Score the edges of the cutlets in a few places to keep the edges from curling during the frying process. Salt and pepper both sides. Dredge in flour, dip into beaten egg and then coat both sides with breadcrumbs.

Fill a heavy pot with about 3in of vegetable oil and heat to 350°F (mark 4). Deep-fry one or two cutlets at a time, for 5 to 7 minutes, turning once or twice. Skim the oil to keep it clean and clear. Remove the cutlets and drain them for a few seconds on absorbent towelling. Slice the pork on the diagonal into ³/₄in wide strips and keep warm.

Wash the trefoil, pat dry and chop coarsely. Slice the onion into rounds, and sauté them in a skillet in a little oil, until soft and translucent. Add the *dashi*, *mirin* and soysauce. Simmer.

Pour the beaten egg into the skillet, then add to it the chopped trefoil. Stir slightly as the egg begins to set. Do not overcook the egg mixture — it should be very moist when you remove the pan from the heat.

Divide the hot rice into four deep bowls and top it with *tonkatsu* strips. Divide the egg mixture into four parts and top the rice and pork with egg. Arrange the egg and the pork strips so that both can be seen.

Juices from both the egg and the cutlet will seep into the rice, making this dish delicious without any further sauces.

TENDON

(*Tempura* on Rice)

IN ANOTHER POPULAR DOMBURI, seafood and vegetables cooked *tempura* style are used as toppings.

Preparation

Score the shrimp a few times crosswise on the underside, to prevent them curling up during deep-frying. Tap the back of each shrimp with the back-edge of a knife. Cut the flattened piece of squid into four. Cut the eggplants into half lengthwise, then into slices ¼in thick.

Heat a generous amount of vegetable oil in a large pot or electric skillet to about 350°F (mark 4). Mix the egg, water and sifted flour as for *tempura* batter. Dredge the shrimp, the squid, the eggplants, the *shishito* peppers and the mushrooms in flour, then in the batter and finally deep-fry in the hot oil (for detailed instructions on cooking *tempura*, see page 138).

Boil the *niban dashi* in a saucepan and add the *mirin* and soy-sauce. Add the *tempura* and simmer for 2 minutes.

Divide the hot rice into four *udon* bowls and top with the *tempura* pieces. Pour the juice over this combination and serve hot.

A small dish of *tsukemono* (Japanese pickles) accompanies this dish perfectly.

INGREDIENTS (Serves 4)
8 shrimp, shucked and
*   deveined*
1 medium sized squid
2 small eggplants
vegetable oil

BATTER:
2 egg yolks
2 cups (16fl.oz) ice-water
2 cups (7oz) sifted flour

8 shishito peppers
4 shiitake mushrooms
flour
2 cups (16fl.oz) niban dashi
4 tbsp mirin
4 tbsp soysauce
8 cups (48oz) hot rice,
*   cooked Japanese style (see*
*   page 94)*

(Illustration overleaf)

■ <u>KATSUDON</u> (page 192)
Pork cutlet on rice
Garnish: *shredded <u>nori</u>*

■ TENDON (page 193)
Tempura on rice

NIGIRI-ZUSHI

('Handful' *sushi*)

INGREDIENTS (Makes 25 portions)
1½ cups (10.5oz) uncooked rice
2½ tbsp sushi-su (sushi vinegar)
1 lb fillet of tuna, skinned
¼ tsp wasabi paste (from ground fresh root and water, or powder and water)
soysauce

(Illustration overleaf)

THIS TOKYO SPECIALTY is one of the most popular dishes among the current generation of foreign lovers of Japanese cuisine. Nothing can equal the quality of *nigiri-zushi* prepared professionally — the Japanese themselves rarely prepare it at home, preferring to order it and have it delivered. Still, there is nothing inherently mysterious about it, and a quite enjoyable version can be made in your own kitchen.

This sort of *sushi* originated on the shore of Tokyo Bay, a body of water that, in the years before industrial pollution, teemed with a great variety of fish. Fishermen preserved their raw catch on beds of vinegared rice. Some genius discovered that the glowingly fresh fish and the rice preservative tasted good together.

Preparation

Cook the rice Japanese style (see page 94) and allow it to cool slightly. In a large, flattish bowl or tub, spread the rice out and sprinkle the *sushi* vinegar over it. Toss the rice with a spoon or rice paddle, while cooling it with a fan. (You may find it easier to ask a friend to fan the rice while you concentrate upon the mixing and tossing.)

Put some cold water into a bowl, add a few drops of vinegar and use the liquid to moisten your hands as you shape the rice into 24 small balls. Pick up a small (1½in) wad of rice and squeeze it gently with your left hand (if you are right-handed). Be careful not to squeeze too hard. With the first two fingers of your right hand, shape and smooth the rice ball, working against the palm of your left hand. When all the rice balls are made, cover them with a damp cloth and set aside. Do not refrigerate.

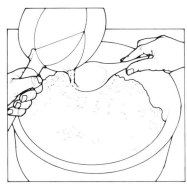

1. *Cook the rice Japanese style and, after it has cooled slightly, place it in a bowl and spread it out. Pour in the sushi vinegar.*

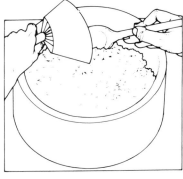

2. *Using a spoon or rice paddle, mix the rice thoroughly with the vinegar, while at the same time cooling it with a fan.*

3. *Mix a few drops of vinegar with some cold water and moisten your hands with the mixture. Pick up a small amount of rice and shape it into a ball.*

With a very sharp knife, slice the tuna fillet crosswise at a slight diagonal, making ⅛in wide slices. Put a little dab of *wasabi* paste on the underside of each slice. (It is better to put on too little than too much; a lot of *wasabi* all at once is a startling experience.) Spread the *wasabi* thinly.

Top each rice-ball with a prepared slice of fish, *wasabi*-side down. Again, cradling the rice ball in your left palm, use your first two fingers to gently press the fish down onto the rice. You may have a couple of broken rice-balls the first time you try, but very soon you will develop the right 'touch' for making neat, compact little *nigiri*.

Serve with a little bowl of dipping sauce (soysauce) for each person. Eat with the fingers, placing your first two fingers on the fish and your thumb underneath the rice ball. Turn upside down and dip the fish lightly in the soysauce; try not to get sauce on the rice — that way you will keep the *nigiri* from crumbling.

Nigiri-zushi is made with many different kinds of raw fish and shellfish. The one requirement, of course, is that the fish be absolutely fresh. If this is not possible, a fine *nigiri* can be made with smoked salmon, sliced thinly and cut into little oblongs, long enough to cover the rice-balls completely.

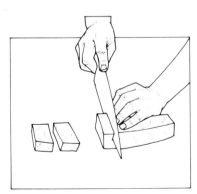

4. Using a very sharp knife, slice the fillet crosswise at a slight angle into slices ⅛in thick.

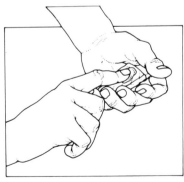

5. Smear a little dab of wasabi on the center of each slice of fish. Be careful to spread the wasabi thinly — it has a very powerful taste.

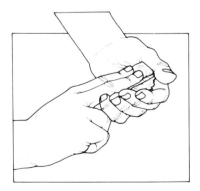

6. Cradling a rice ball in one hand, place a fish slice wasabi-side down onto the ball. Press down gently, using index and middle fingers.

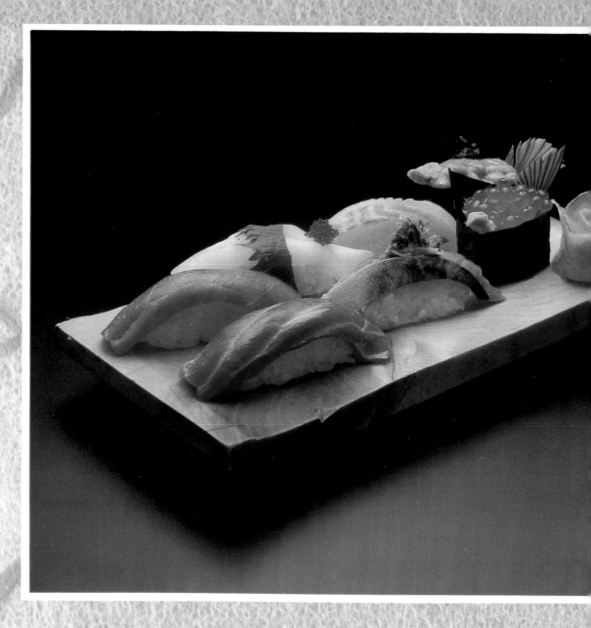

■ NIGIRI-ZUSHI (page 194)
Vinegared rice and seafood:
Tuna, squid, shrimp and starfish (left to right, back row)
Tuna, mackerel, salmon roe (left to right, front row)
Garnish: *pickled ginger*

■ NIGIRI-ZUSHI (page 194)
Shrimp and lemon slices on vinegared rice decorated
with shrimp tails (top)
Sea bass on vinegared rice (bottom)

THE NORTH

*T*his is a vast area stretching from the edge of the Kantō Plain all the way to the northernmost tip of Japan's northernmost island, Hokkaidō. People from this area share a similar outlook on life — a down-to-earth and no-nonsense quality based, perhaps, upon the fact that conditions in the North have always been difficult. Japan's highest mountains run up the spine of north Honshū, and the Japan Sea side of the region is one of the snowiest places on earth. As far as Japanese cuisine is concerned, this region is famous for its stews and warming one-pots.

WHEN THE GREAT seventeenth century poet Matsuo Bashō passed the military barrier at the Shirakawa Pass and headed north on his famous poetry-writing journey, he entered a vast region that, for many Japanese of his day, was as unknown as a foreign country. The Tōhoku, or North-East, began just beyond the capital city of Edo (Tokyo) and comprised the two feudatories of Mutsu and Dewa. And beyond the northernmost point of Tōhoku lay the vast, uncharted island named Ezo, with its semi-barbarous native people. The Matsumae feudal house kept a precarious Japanese toehold on the southernmost extremity of this trackless region. On his travels, Bashō records that he found large parts truly desolate and wild, far removed from the familiar, overpopulated, and perhaps overcivilized Kansai heartland.

Today, the north of Japan has been transformed in many ways. The two feudatories of the Tōhoku have become four prefectures; Ezo has been re-christened Hokkaidō, and the native people — the Ainu — are a nearly extinct race, sadly reduced to giving 'authentic' bear dances for tourists and carving wooden trinkets. American-

Salmon and trout (inset) play an important part in the cooking of the north, where the the north, where the independence of the inhabitants is reflected in the straightforwardness of their diet. Beyond Lake Inawashiro (left) rise the peaks of the Bandai massif, on the northern side of which is a group of over 100 small lakes, formed by a huge volcanic eruption in 1888.

The cliffs at Kitayamazaki (above), on the north-east tip of Honshu, are part of the Rikuchu-kaigan National Park, one of 27 such parks all over the country conserving areas of great national beauty.

The tower and old bridge of Tsuguru Castle at cherry blossom time in Hirosaki (center), one of the main towns of north-west Honshu.

style farming methods, introduced in the Meiji Period (1868-1912), have transformed Hokkaidō into a major producer of non-traditional crops and products: milk, cheese, Western vegetables and Indian corn. The Tōhoku remains what it has been for several generations, the 'rice bowl' of the nation, where 20 percent of the national crop is grown. Northern politicians in the ruling Liberal Democratic Party have done handsomely by their constituents — a recently-completed 'Bullet Train' to the Tōhoku speeds travelers into the 'deep North' in a fraction of the time that it took Bashō to make his pilgrimage.

Still, however, the North remains definably 'different' from the rest of the nation. The weather (especially on the snowy Japan Sea side) is more severe; and the region's poverty has produced a toughness, a resilience, and an impatience with over-refinement, that distinguish Northerners from other Japanese. When they eat,

they like copious quantity, good taste, and an atmosphere free of affectation. *Soba* noodles, made of buckwheat, are a particular favorite, as are *nabemono*, hearty stews full of the seafood of the region.

The cuisine of Hokkaidō is an interesting variant on the northern pattern. Here the curly Chinese *ramen* noodle is at its best, fine beer is brewed, and such innovations as asparagus and Irish potatoes enrich Japanese eating. Hokkaidō's pride, however, is its salmon, which is famous all over the country, and is enjoyed in many forms by local people.

The cooking of the North reminds us in a special way of the quintessential characteristics of all Japanese cuisine — the emphasis on freshness and, despite elaborations for the eye, an essential simplicity. These characteristics emerge, in perhaps their most accessible forms, in the simple, hearty dishes of the North.

Toshogu Shrine (top) is the most important at Nikko. Its buildings are lavishly decorated in a style that could almost be called Rococo. The city of Sendai celebrates the Tanabata Festival (above) in grand style on August 7th. It celebrates the love of two stars which could only meet once a year. Strips of colored paper are inscribed with the love poems of the hopeful.

HOTATE-GAI SHOYO YAKI

(Scallops Broiled in Soysauce)

INGREDIENTS (Serves 4)
4 to 8 scallops
2 tbsp sake
2 tbsp soysauce
4 lemon wedges
parsley

(Illustration overleaf)

帆
立
貝
醤
油
焼
き

A POPULAR PARTY DISH all over Japan, this dish comes from Hokkaidō where there are many little food stalls that sell this tasty, seafood snack.

Preparation

Clean the scallops carefully and, with a sharp knife, separate the meat from the shells. If the scallops are large, cut them into 1in sections. Taking four shells, distribute the scallops equally among them and pour ½ tbsp *sake* and ½ tbsp soysauce over the scallops in each shell.

Put the shells on a charcoal fire and broil for a few minutes, or until the scallops are cooked and not too hard. Serve the scallops hot in the shells garnished with a lemon wedge and parsley.

SAKE NO OYAKO-MUSHI

(Steamed Salmon with Roe)

INGREDIENTS (Serves 4)
1 lb salmon fillets, boned and
  skinned
vegetable oil
4 tbsp salmon roe
2 tbsp sake
1 cup (4oz) grated daikon
  (white radish)
½ egg white, lightly beaten
salt
1 cup (8fl.oz) ichiban dashi
3 tbsp mirin
2 tbsp rice vinegar
2 tbsp light soysauce (if
  unavailable, use dark)
2 tsp cornstarch, mixed with
  2 tsp water into a paste
1 lemon

(Illustration overleaf)

鮭
の
親
子
蒸
し

TŌHOKU SALMON is the finest and most famous in the nation, and Tōhoku people are particularly fond of eating it in combination with its roe. Note the similarity between this dish and *tai no shinshu-mushi* (see opposite); in both, a regional ingredient is added to the fish, and steamed with it to impart a characteristic flavor.

Preparation

Cut the salmon fillets into very thin slices. Lightly oil a skillet and sauté the salmon briefly, about 1½ minutes per side, over a medium heat. Rinse the pieces carefully with cold water, using a colander. Place the pieces, evenly divided, into four heatproof bowls.

Place the roe in a small bowl and mix it with the *sake* to clean it; then strain and discard the liquid. Set aside.

Mix the grated *daikon* with the beaten egg white in another bowl, then scatter a pinch of salt over the *daikon* and egg. Add the roe and toss. Spoon the roe, egg and *daikon* mixture over the pieces of fish.

Cover the bowls securely with foil or plastic wrap, place in a hot steamer and steam for 5 minutes over a high heat.

Mix the *dashi*, *mirin*, vinegar and soysauce in a small saucepan and bring the mixture to the boil. Pour in the paste of water and cornstarch and stir over a medium-high heat until the mixture becomes thicker and glossy. Remove from the heat.

Remove the bowls from the steamer, uncover, and top each bit of fish and roe with some of the sauce. Complete with a squeeze of lemon-juice on each portion. Serve hot.

TAI NO SHINSŪ-MUSHI

(Steamed Japan Alps Fish)

SEA-BREAM, the celebratory fish, is here deliciously combined with *soba* noodles in a recipe that comes from the mountainous central region of northern Honshū.

Preparation

Fillet the fish using the *sanmai-oroshi* technique (see page 30). Divide each of the boneless fillets in half crosswise, salt lightly and leave to rest at room temperature for about 40 minutes. Wash and pat dry with kitchen towelling.

Add the noodles to a saucepan of boiling water, separating them as they go in. Let the water return to the boil then add a cup (8fl.oz.) of cold water. Allow to return to the boil then add a second cup of cold water. When the water boils once more, remove from the heat and drain the noodles thoroughly.

Wipe the *konbu* with a lightly-dampened cloth and divide into four pieces. Place the *konbu* pieces into the bottom of four heatproof bowls.

On top of the seaweed, place even portions of the noodles, and on top of the noodles, the four pieces of fish, skin-side-up. Splash 1 tbsp of *sake* on each piece of fish.

Cover each bowl *tightly* with foil or plastic wrap and place in a hot steamer. Steam over a high heat for 10 minutes.

Combine the *dashi, mirin* and soysauce and bring to a rapid boil. Stir in the bonito flakes and strain right away. Discard the flakes.

Remove the bowls from the steamer, and top each portion with the hot sauce. Garnish with the chopped green onions and shreds of *nori* seaweed.

INGREDIENTS (Serves 4)

1 sea bream
¼ lb dried soba noodles
    (green cha-soba are
    particularly attractive —
    see page 27)
4 × 6in piece of konbu (kelp)
4 tbsp sake
1²/₃ cups (14fl.oz) ichiban
    dashi
6 tbsp mirin
6 tbsp soysauce
1 cup (2oz) dried bonito
    flakes (katsuo-bushi)
½ cup (2oz) chopped green
    onions
1 sheet nori seaweed

■ HOTATE-GAI SHOYU YAKI (page 204)
Scallops broiled in soysauce
Garnish: *parsley and lemon slices*

■ SAKE NO OYAKO-MUSHI (page 204)
Steamed salmon with roe
Garnish: *sansho leaf*

NISHIN NO NITSUKE

(Simmered Herring)

INGREDIENTS (Serves 4)
2 potatoes
2 herring, cleaned
1 cup (8fl.oz) ichiban dashi
½ cup (4fl.oz) sake
½ cup (4fl.oz) mirin
½ cup (4fl.oz) soysauce
3in square piece of konbu,
*   cut into 4 strips*
1 tbsp shredded fresh ginger

(Illustration overleaf)

鰊
煮
つ
け

THE FINEST HERRING come from northern waters. Kansai cooks traditionally use dried herring in their recipes, commemorating the days when the fish had to be transported over long distances to them. This northern recipe, however, uses the fresh variety in a standard, delicious *nimono*.

Preparation

Peel and dice the potatoes and cut into 1in cubes. Boil in slightly salty water, till tender but not flaky, then drain well.

Cut boneless fillets using the *sanmai-oroshi* technique (see page 30); do not skin. Blanch the fillets for about 30 seconds in boiling water. Drain, wash in cold water and pat dry.

Combine the *dashi, sake, mirin*, soysauce and *konbu* in a small saucepan and simmer.

Add the herring fillets, skin-side-up and, using a drop-lid (*otoshi-buta*), simmer over a very low heat for 20 to 30 minutes.

Remove the saucepan from the heat and carefully cut the fillets into thirds. Place the fillets on individual serving dishes, dividing the pieces equally, and keep warm.

Remove the *konbu* from the pan of simmering sauce, cut into four strips and reserve. Place the boiled potatoes in the remaining simmering liquid. Cover with a drop lid and simmer over a low heat for 10 minutes or until the potatoes are cooked. Add the potatoes to the fish, and top both with the remaining liquid. Garnish with shreds of ginger and the *konbu* strips.

TORI JIBU-NI

(Chicken Simmered Dish)

INGREDIENTS (Serves 4)
12oz boned chicken
6 leaves Chinese white
*   cabbage*
all-purpose flour
1 cup (8fl.oz) ichiban dashi
4 tbsp light soysauce (if
*   unavailable, use dark)*
4 tbsp mirin
1 tbsp sugar
½ tsp wasabi paste

鶏
じ
ぶ
煮

STRIPS OF CHINESE CABBAGE and chicken are simmered separately, but are eaten together, served with a dab of *wasabi*.

Preparation

Cut the chicken into 2in pieces and dredge lightly in flour.

Separate the Chinese cabbage leaves, keeping them whole. Bring an ample amount of lightly salted water to the boil in a large pot and boil the cabbage leaves for 3 to 4 minutes. Drain thoroughly.

Lay out each leaf separately and cut them into small strips: cut evenly three times crosswise, then seven times lengthwise. Return the leaves to the empty cooking pot.

In another pot, mix the *dashi*, soysauce, *mirin* and sugar. Bring to the boil, reduce the heat and simmer for 2 minutes. Then pour two-thirds of this liquid over the cabbage strips in the first pot, bring to the boil, reduce the heat slightly, and gently boil the cabbage for 10 minutes.

In the second pot, in which a third of the simmering mixture remains, place the chicken strips. Simmer over a medium heat until most of the liquid is absorbed by the chicken (about 8 to 10 minutes).

In individual serving dishes, make small mounds of the cooked cabbage strips, and top each with pieces of chicken, arranged neatly. Add a little of the remaining cabbage liquid to each serving, and give each person a tiny cone of *wasabi* paste so that they can season their own food.

KAKI-MISO

(Oysters in *Miso*)

TWO PRODUCTS of which the Japanese of the Tōhoku region are right-fully proud — oysters and bean paste — combine in this interestingly-flavored dish.

Preparation

Rinse the oysters thoroughly in cold water. Plunge them into a generous amount of boiling water and blanch them for approximately 30 seconds. Drain.

Trim the green onions and blanch them, likewise, in boiling salted water for 30 seconds. Drain, pat dry with kitchen towelling, and cut into 1½in segments.

Mix the *miso*, vinegar and sugar in a saucepan and heat gently, stirring with a wooden or plastic spoon. Add the oysters and simmer briefly, for about 2 minutes; then toss in the cut green onions and allow the mixture to return to room temperature. Serve.

INGREDIENTS (Serves 4)
牡 *1 lb oysters, shucked*
蠣 *6-7 green onions*
味 *6 tbsp Sendai miso (dark*
噌 *bean paste)*
6 tbsp sugar
4 tbsp rice wine vinegar

(Illustration overleaf)

■ <u>NISHIN NO NITSUKE</u> (page 208)
Simmered herring
Garnish: *bonito flakes*

■ KAKI-MISO (page 209)
Oysters in _miso_
Garnish: _sansho leaf_

YOSENABE

(Seafood and Vegetable One-Pot)

寄
せ
鍋

NABEMONO — one-pot meals — are a real favorite of Northerners, and *yosenabe* epitomizes the kind of hearty *nabemono* they like to eat.

Preparation

Chop the chicken breast into bite-sized pieces. Boil the spinach in lightly salted water, until just limp and the color darkens. Boil the Chinese cabbage leaves till tender, about 2 to 4 minutes. Cut the egg roll into six slices. Cut the *naganegi* diagonally into thin slices. Soak the *harusame* filaments in warm water for 5 minutes, then drain.

On a large platter or wooden dish, make an attractive arrangement of all the ingredients: the chicken pieces, spinach, Chinese cabbage leaves, *naganegi* slices (sliced green onions can be used as a substitute), *harusame*, shrimp, *enokidake* mushrooms, chrysanthemum leaves, *konnyaku* slices, ginkgo nuts, salmon, turbot and squid slices.

Using a heating unit on the table, heat the *ichiban dashi* and the *konbu* in a large pot and bring to the boil. Discard the *konbu*. Add the soysauce, *sake* and salt, lower the heat and keep at simmering point.

Everybody takes their pick of the ingredients on the platter and cooks them for a few minutes in the bubbling stock. Be careful not to overcrowd the cooking pot.

INGREDIENTS (Serves 6)
1 whole chicken breast
½ lb spinach
6 large Chinese cabbage leaves
1 egg roll (see page 62)
1 naganegi (or a bunch of thick green onions)
2oz harusame (vermicelli)
6 shrimp, shucked and deveined
1 bunch of enokidake mushrooms
½ lb shungiku (young chrysanthemum leaves)
1 cake konnyaku, sliced into 6
6 gingko nuts
2 slices salmon
2 slices turbot
2 slices squid

FOR THE STOCK:
4 cups (32fl.oz) ichiban dashi
4in piece of konbu
4 tbsp soysauce
2 tbsp sake
1 tsp salt

(Illustration overleaf)

ASUPARAGASU KARASHI-ZUKE

(Spicy Asparagus)

ASPARAGUS IS ONE of the non-traditional crops grown on large farms on the northernmost island of Hokkaidō. As with so many other new products (beef, wine grapes, apples), the Japanese farmers have contrived to produce some of the finest examples of asparagus in the world. This dish, a salad, combines this foreign vegetable with a semi-traditional seasoning.

Preparation

Cut the asparagus into 1½in sections and boil in lightly salted water. While the asparagus is still crisp, remove and rinse in cold water.

In a large bowl, combine the mustard with the water and mix thoroughly. Add the egg yolk and blend, then the soysauce; mix all the ingredients well.

Add the asparagus to the mixing bowl and toss. Serve in small individual dishes, arranging the asparagus pieces attractively.

INGREDIENTS (Serves 4)
20 spears of asparagus, trimmed
pinch of salt
2 tsp powdered mustard (Western type)
2 tsp water
1 egg yolk
1 tsp soysauce

KURI-MESHI

(Chestnut Rice)

IN JAPAN, chestnuts appear on the market in late September. This dish is a fall favorite throughout the country.

Preparation

If you are using fresh chestnuts, shuck them and remove the inner skin, using a small, sharp knife. Cut the nuts in halves or quarters, depending on their size. If you are using the bottled variety, drain thoroughly and halve the chestnuts. Try to avoid crumbling them. Rinse the chestnuts thoroughly in cold water. Peel the ginkgo nuts (for instructions, see page 23) and chop them in half.

Dissolve the salt in the water. Place the rice in a cooking vessel or automatic rice cooker and pour the salt-water over the rice. Add the chestnuts and ginkgo nuts. Cook according to the general instructions for rice (see page 94); be sure to let the rice stand for 15 minutes, covered, before serving. Serve hot in individual bowls. Give each diner his or her share of chestnut pieces and ginkgo nuts.

INGREDIENTS (Serves 4)
15 large, fresh chestnuts or 4 7oz bottles of yellow chestnuts (available in Oriental markets)
8 ginkgo nuts
½ tsp salt
4 cups (32fl.oz) water
3½ cups (22oz) short-grain rice

(Illustration overleaf)

SOBA

(Buckwheat Noodles)

SOBA ARE ENJOYED from one end of Japan to the other, but they are at their best in the North, where they originated. The recipe here is one of the most delicious of the many ways to serve buckwheat noodles.

Preparation

To make the dipping sauce, combine the *dashi*, soysauce, *mirin* and sugar in a saucepan and heat enough so that the sugar dissolves. Then chill the sauce.

Fill a large pot three-quarters full with cold water and bring to a high boil. Add the noodles, separating them as they go in. Allow the water to return to the boil, then add a cup (8fl.oz) of cold water. Allow to return to the boil, then add a second cup (8fl.oz) of cold water. When the water boils once more, remove from the heat, drain the noodles, chill and serve them on four plates or in small bamboo baskets.

Place the condiments — the green onions and *wasabi* — in small separate dishes, and give each person a small bowl of dipping sauce. Pass the *nori* seaweed over an open flame, dry-roasting it for about 1 minute total, then crumble the sheet over the mounds of noodles as a garnish. To eat, season the dipping sauce with condiments according to taste, and dip the noodles into the sauce.

INGREDIENTS (Serves 4)
1½ cups (12fl.oz) ichiban dashi
3 tbsp soysauce
1 tbsp mirin
1½ tbsp sugar
4 portions dried soba (total of about 24oz)
½ sheet dried nori seaweed
¼ cup (1oz) green onions
2 tsp wasabi paste

(Illustration overleaf)

■ <u>YOSENABE</u> (page 212)
Seafood and vegetable one-pot
Garnish: *'flower-cut' carrots and decorative fu*

■ <u>CHA-SOBA</u> (page 213)
Green-tea <u>*soba*</u> noodles
Garnish: <u>*nori shreds*</u>
(Illustration opposite top)

■ <u>KURI-MESHI</u> (page 213)
Chestnut rice
Garnish: *small bunch of trefoil*
(Illustration opposite bottom)

USEFUL ADDRESSES

JAPANESE FOOD SHOPS IN THE UNITED STATES OF AMERICA

NORTH CALIFORNIA

ABC Fish and Oriental Food
1911 Portrero Way
Sacramento 95822

Asahi Market
5616 Thornton Ave.
Newark 94560

Asahi Ya
229 East Alpine Avenue
Stockton 95009

Dobashi Company
240 E. Jackson St.
San Jose 95112

International Market
2019 Fillmore Street
San Francisco 94115

Kenson Trading
1251 Stockton Street
San Francisco 94133

Miko's Japanese Foods
524 Tuolumne
Vallejo 94590

Nishioka Fish Market
665 N. Sixth St.
San Jose 95112

Nomura Market
29583 Mission Blvd.
Hayward 94544

The Omodaka
115 Clement Street
San Francisco 94118

K. Sakai Co. (Uoki)
1656 Post Street
San Francisco 94115

Sanwa Market
2122 Cabrillo St.
San Francisco 94121

Suruki
140 Boothbay
Foster City 94404

Takahashi Company
221 S. Claremont St.
San Mateo 94401

SOUTH CALIFORNIA

Asahi Company
660 Oxnard Blvd.
Oxnard 93030

Ebisu Market
18940 Brookhurst St.
Fountain Valley 92708

Eiko Shoten
6082 University Ave.
San Diego 92115

Fujiya Market
601 N. Virgil Ave.
Los Angeles 90004

Fukuda's
2412 S. Escondido Blvd.
Escondido 92025

Motoyama Market
16135 S. Western Ave.
Gardena 90247

New Meiji Market
1620 W. Redondo Beach
Gardena 90247

Nippon Foods
2935 West Ball Road
Anaheim 92804

Omori's
2700 N. Santa Fe
Vista 92083

Sakae Oriental Grocery
4277 Convoy St.
San Diego 92111

S & N Food Market
2600 E. 1st Street
Los Angeles 90033

Senri Market
111 N. Lincoln Ave.
Monterey Park 91754

Yamamoto Bros
314 Wilmington Blvd.
Wilmington 90744

ILLINOIS

Diamond Trading Co.
913 W. Belmont Ave.
Chicago 60657

Furuya & Company
5358 N. Clark St.
Chicago 60640

Star Market
3349 N. Clark St.
Chicago 60657

NEW YORK

Harumi
318-320 W. 231 St.
Bronx 10463

Katagiri Company
224 East 59th St.
New York 10022

Meidiya
18 N. Central Park Ave.
Hartsdale 10530

Tanaka & Company
326 Amsterdam Ave.
New York 10023

Tokyo Sales Corp.
142 W. 57th St.
New York 10019

TEXAS

Edoya Oriental
223 Farmer Branch
Dallas 75234

Japanese Grocery
14366-B Memorial Dr.
Houston 77079

Nippon Daido Int'l
11138 Westheimer
Houston 77042

Tachibana
4886 Hercules Ave.
El Paso 79904

JAPANESE FOOD SHOPS IN CANADA

BRITISH COLUMBIA

Mihamaya
392 Powell St.
Vancouver B.C.

Shimizu Shoten
349 East Hasting St.
Vancouver B.C.

ONTARIO

Furuya Trading Co. Ltd.
460 Dundas St. West
Toronto
Ontario

Iwaki Japanese Food Store
2627 Yonge St.
Toronto
Ontario

Nakanishi Japan Food Store
465 Somerset St. West
Ottawa
Ontario

Sanko Trading Co.
221 Spadina Ave.
Toronto
Ontario

Yanagawa Japanese Foods
639 Upper James St.
Hamilton
Ontario

QUEBEC

Miyamoto Provisions
382 Victoria Ave.
Montreal Westmount
Quebec

JAPANESE RESTAURANTS IN LONDON

Ajimura
51-53 Shelton Street
Covent Garden
London WC2
Tel: 01 240-0178

Restaurant Asuka
Berkeley Arcade
209a Baker Street
London NW1
Tel: 01 486-5026

Aykoku-Kaku
Bucklersbury House
9 Walbrook
London EC4
Tel: 01 236-9020

Azami
13 West Street
London WC2
Tel: 01 240-0634

Defune
(sushi restaurant)
61 Blandford Street
London W1
Tel: 01 935-8311

Fuji
36 Brewer Street
London W1
Tel: 01 734-0957

Hama-Yakiniku
253 Finchley Road
London NW3
Tel: 01 794-1723

Hanaguruma
49 Bow Lane
London EC4
Tel: 01 236-6451

Hiroko at Kensington Hilton
179-199 Holland Park Avenue
London W11
Tel: 01 603-5003

Hokkai
59 Brewer Street
London W1
Tel: 01 734-5826

Ikeda
30 Brook Street
London W1
Tel: 01 629-2730

Kiku
12 Whitehorse Street
Shepherd Market
London W1
Tel: 01 499-4208/9

Kyoto
Central Park Hotel
74-76 Queensborough Terrace
London W2
Tel: 01 221-5843

Kitchen Yakitori
12 Lancashire Court
New Bond Street
London W1
Tel: 01 629-9984

Masako/Sushi Masa
6-8 St Christopher's Place
London W1
Tel: 01 935-1579

Mikado
110 George Street
London W1
Tel: 01 935-8320

Mima
John Howard Hotel
4 Queensgate
London SW7
Tel: 01 581-3832

Nanten/Yakitori Bar
6-8 Blandford Street London
W1
Tel: 01 935-6319

Ninjin Ltd (Restaurant group)
77 Baker Street
London W1
Tel: 01 486-9843

Saga
43 South Molton Street
London W1
Tel: 01 408-2236

Sakura
9 Hanover Street
London W1
Tel: 01 629-2961

Suntory
72 St James's Street
London SW1
Tel: 01 499-7993

Yamaju
16 Beak Street
London W1
Tel: 01 437-2236

JAPANESE FOOD SHOPS IN LONDON

Furusato Foods
67A Camden High Street
London NW1
Tel: 01 388-3979

J. A. Centre
348-356 Regents Park Road
Finchley Central
London N3
Tel: 01 346-1042

J. A. Centre
250 Upper Richmond Road
London SW15
Tel: 01 789-3980

Japanese Publication Centre, Food Section
5 Warwick Street
London W1
Tel: 01 437-4480

Mikadoya
193 Upper Richmond Road
London SW5
Tel: 01 788-3905

Mitsukiku
90 Regent Street
London W1
Tel: 01 437-5582

Mitsukiku
157 Victoria Street
London SW1
Tel: 01 828-0158

Ninjin
224 Great Portland Street
London W1
Tel: 01 388-2511

Nippon Food Centre
483 Finchley Road
London NW3
Tel: 01 794-2933

Tokyo-ya
20 North End Road
Golders Green
London NW11
Tel: 01 458-8333

Yamatoya
55 Church Road
Hendon
London NW4
Tel: 01 203-4773

JAPANESE BOOKSHOPS IN LONDON

Japan Publications Centre
5 Warwick Street
London W1
Tel: 01 439-8035

Books Nippon
64-66 St Paul's Churchyard
London EC4
Tel: 01 248-4956

Nihon Token-do
23 Museum Street
London WC1
Tel: 01 580-6511

INDEX

*'Let little seem like much, as long
as it is fresh, natural and beautiful'*

THE PHILOSOPHY OF JAPANESE CUISINE